LAST MINUTE SYSTEM DESIGN INTERVIEWS

Must Learn Topics With Real World Examples

Gopala Krishna Murty Nanduri

INDIA · SINGAPORE · MALAYSIA

ISBN 979-8-89277-885-5

Contents

Chapter 1

Overview

System design round has become one of the most important rounds for almost every software engineering interview these days. In fact it's one of the key factors that decides your position and salary level the company offers you.

So, do you think you are fully prepared to crack your upcoming system design interview round? If not, you are in the right place to learn. There are tons of resources over the web to learn about system design interviews. But this book collects the central concepts that you need to learn for your next system design interview and even if you are preparing for system design at the last minute, reading through the concepts of this book should get you best at your system design rounds.

By the end of this book, you will be interview ready to crack system design interviews that involves:

1. Get a very good picture of how real world systems work and how they interact end to end.
2. Design a high level end to end system and how you can scale it to the next level with the core concepts required.
3. A Must learn hand picked list of most frequently asked important System design interview questions and solutions that you can apply for any new question that is asked in the interview

So what are you waiting for? Bring in your passion and use this book to full extent to crack your next system design interview.

How is this book organized?

This book is structured into 9 different chapters.

Chapter 1: is the basic overview which you are currently reading.

Chapter 2: deals with System design interviews overview and what to expect in these interviews. Also introduces a simple and handy **READ** technique to approach system design interviews.

Chapter 3: deals with System design basics. These basics are important concepts that you need to learn to be successful in the software industry. So try to learn these concepts in depth before diving into other chapters.

Chapters 4 - 9: A total of 6 different must learn interview questions covering various kinds of use cases for distributed system design. Each question is different in its own way of design. So try to read them as much as possible.

How to get the best out of this book?

Don't read this book just like any other textbook. Instead try to follow below tips for maximum benefit from this book.

1. **Think about how you would design your own website/app**
    - Before diving into the book's content, imagine you are the CEO/CTO of your own company and want to build your startup. Now you want to design your own app / website for any topic. For example, think of designing your own

version of facebook, twitter, or any small website idea of your choice.

- First try to brainstorm your thoughts on a piece of paper or whiteboard on how you would do system design for your app. What if your app has thousands of users to begin with. Now try to read this book so that you will learn the topics more efficiently.

2. **Problem-Centric Learning**
    - As you navigate through the chapters, don't just passively absorb information. Actively engage with the content by contemplating the problems posed and formulating your own solutions before reading the provided answers.
    - This problem-centric approach encourages critical thinking and helps solidify your understanding of the underlying concepts. It also prepares you for the type of reasoning required during actual system design interviews.

3. **Relate System Design to Everyday Life**
    - System design is not an abstract concept; instead it mirrors real-life situations. As you explore topics like queues, databases, and load balancing, draw parallels with everyday scenarios. Think about how queues work in a cafe or how a librarian manages books in a large library in the form of a database.
    - By associating these technical concepts with tangible examples, you create mental connections that enhance your ability to recall and apply them in interviews.

4. **Take Notes**
    - Make it a habit to take detailed notes as you progress through the book. Jot down key concepts, design patterns, and any insights that stand out to you.
    - The act of note-taking not only reinforces your memory but also serves as a valuable reference when revisiting the material. Your notes can be a quick review before interviews and a personalized study guide.
5. **Apply Your Knowledge**
    - Put theory into practice by designing systems independently. Select a random website or application and sketch out its architecture. Compare your solution with the examples and solutions provided in the book.
    - This hands-on approach helps bridge the gap between theoretical understanding and practical application, making you more confident and adept in tackling system design challenges.

Preparing system design interviews in Last Minute?

In the fast-paced world of interviews, time is critical and every minute counts. So if you are rushing for interview preparation go through at least the next three to four chapters of this book which are your key to swiftly acquiring the essential knowledge required to excel in system design interviews.

These main key chapters for last minute preparation include:

Chapter 1: System Design Interview Introduction

- Familiarize yourself with the importance of the system design round in today's software engineering interviews. This chapter provides a unique **READ** technique to approach system design interviews. Read through this technique and look at some of the must learn important interview questions in the following chapters.

Chapter 2: System Design Basics

- Quickly dive into the foundational aspects of system design. This chapter provides a rapid yet comprehensive overview of the basics you need to grasp before heading into your interview. Going through these topics can help you deal with most technical aspects that you might face in your interview. Right balance and depth has been chosen to explain these concepts with examples.

Chapter 3: Must Learn Important Interview Question (URL shortener service)

- Dive into the basic chapter focusing on the design of a URL shortener service. This practical scenario will deepen your understanding of system design concepts within the context of a real-world application.

Note that there are a total of 6 different types of problems discussed in the book (Must learn important interview questions 1 to 6). Each question is unique and its own challenges in scaling and building large scale systems. It's better to go through each of these questions, but if you are preparing at the last minute try reading through at least 2 system design questions.

Study plans for last minute system design interview preparation

Here are two study plans that you can follow for last minute system design interview preparation.

1 Week Study plan

If you are really in a rush to prepare for system design interviews and want to get a decent grip of system design concepts, you can use the below 1 week study plan. Please note every person's situation and knowledge can be different. Depending on the reading speed this can about 7 to 10 days. So plan your preparation accordingly.

Day 1: System Design Introduction

Spend the first day reviewing the *system design interview introduction* chapter from this book, including steps such as requirement analysis, clarifications, and system capacity estimation.

Day 2: System Design Basics

Dive into the *system design basics chapter*, focusing on key concepts such as the lifecycle of a web request, distributed systems core concepts, high availability, reliability, fault tolerance, performance, load balancing, caching, queues, storage systems, architecture patterns, and consistent hashing. We strongly recommend reading through this chapter before jumping into practice questions.

Day 3: Must Learn Important Interview Questions 1

On the third day, shift your focus to the first important interview question i.e. **chapter: Must Learn Important Interview Question 1** Review the requirements, estimation of system capacity, API and model design, detailed design and scalability for each question. Read through the chapters and go through all the approaches mentioned in the chapter.

Day 4: Must Learn Important Interview Question 2 & 3

Any left over content from the previous day, Spend this day diving into **Must Learn Important Interview Question 2 and Must Learn Important Interview Question 3**. Review and practice solving these questions, ensuring you understand the structured approach outlined in the book.

Tip: Read one chapter perfectly rather than rushing to complete multiple chapters. Learn and apply that concepts to any new question that you may be asked.

Day 5: Practice Whiteboarding Session

One of the most important things to do in any interview preparation is to practice. Engage in a whiteboarding session either with a study partner or on your own. Choose any question from **Must Learn Important Interview Question** 4, 5, or 6 and practice solving it on a whiteboard. Afterward, review your solution in the respective chapters and seek feedback for improvement from your study partner.

Day 6: One more whiteboarding session

Digest the feedback from the previous day and focus on practicing one more interview question on a whiteboard or a book. You can choose one of the **Must Learn Important Interview questions** 4, 5 or 6 outlined in this book. Review the requirements, refine your problem-solving approach, and practice articulating your solution clearly and concisely.

Day 7: Review and Other Activities

Review all the topics that you practiced so far in Day 1-6 and focus on your weak areas. Read these topics again in the book or online to master them.

This refined one-week plan prioritizes system design basics at the beginning, followed by focused practice on interview questions and whiteboarding sessions. Adjust the schedule as needed based on your specific priorities and available time. Good luck with your preparation!

20 day Study plan

Day 1: System Design Introduction

Review the system design interview introduction chapter, focusing on **READ** technique for Requirement analysis, Estimations, API and model design, High level design and scalability.

Day 2: System design basics

Dive into system design basics starting with

1. Lifecycle of a Web Request
    - Start by reading about the lifecycle of a web request, understanding the various stages involved from the client's request to the server's response.
    - Take note of important concepts such as request processing, middleware, and response generation.
2. Distributed Systems Core Concepts
    - Dive into the core concepts of distributed systems, including definitions and characteristics of distributed systems.

- Understand concepts such as scalability, reliability, fault tolerance, and consistency in distributed systems.

Day 3: Exploring Load Balancer, Caching, and Queues

1. Load Balancer
   - Learn about load balancing techniques and their importance in distributed systems.
   - Understand different load balancing algorithms and their use cases.
2. Caching
   - Explore caching mechanisms and their role in improving system performance.
   - Understand caching strategies, cache eviction policies, and cache consistency.
3. Queues
   - Study queueing systems and their significance in distributed systems architecture.
   - Learn about different types of queues, such as message queues and task queues, and their applications.

Day 4: Understanding Polling, Long Polling, Websockets and more

1. Polling, Long Polling, Websockets, Server-Sent Events
   - Explore communication protocols and mechanisms such as polling, long polling, Websockets, and Server-Sent Events.
   - Understand their advantages, use cases, and differences.
2. Storage Systems

   Dive into storage systems architecture, including databases, file systems, and distributed storage systems.

- Understand the principles of data storage, replication, sharding, and consistency models.

3. Architecture Patterns

   - Explore common architecture patterns used in distributed systems design, such as Layered Architecture, Microservices, and Event-Driven Architecture.
   - Understand the principles, advantages, and challenges associated with each architecture pattern.

Day 5-7: Must-Learn Interview Questions 1 & 2

- Day 5-6: Focus on the first important interview question outlined in your book. Review requirements, estimate system capacity, and design APIs and models, detailed design and scalability.
- Day 7: Practice solving the second interview question and articulate your solution clearly and concisely.

Day 8-10: Must-Learn Interview Questions 3 & 4

- Day 8-9: Delve into the third important interview question. Review requirements, estimate system capacity, and explore high-level design.
- Day 10: Practice solving the fourth interview question and refine your problem-solving approach.

Day 11-12: Practice Whiteboarding Session

- Day 11: Engage in a whiteboarding session, either alone or with a study partner. Choose a question from the interview questions and practice solving it on a whiteboard.
- Day 12: Review your solution, seek feedback for improvement, and refine your problem-solving skills.

Day 13-15: Must-Learn Interview Questions 5 & 6

- Day 13-14: Focus on the fifth important interview question.
- Day 15: Practice solving the fifth interview question and ensure your solution addresses scalability and extensibility.

Day 16-18: Review and Additional Preparation

- Day 16-17: Use these days for comprehensive review. Revisit key concepts, problem-solving techniques, and interview question solutions.
- Day 18: Engage in additional preparation activities such as mock interviews, further review, or relaxation techniques to build confidence.

Day 19-20: Final Review and Confidence Building

- Day 19: Review all topics covered so far and focus on your weak areas. Read these topics again in the book or online to master them.
- Day 20: Visualize yourself confidently explaining solutions, handling challenging questions, and impressing interviewers with your expertise. Build a positive mindset, trust in your preparation, and take time to relax and recharge before your interviews.

This 20-day plan provides a structured approach to last-minute preparation for system design interviews, focusing on understanding key concepts, solving important interview questions, and practicing problem-solving techniques. Adjust the schedule as needed based on your specific priorities and available time. Good luck with your preparation!

Chapter 2

System design Interview introduction

We use a lot of websites everyday like Google, facebook, twitter and so on right! Let's say your job is to design one such system or a website of that sort.

How would you actually do it ? This is the primary goal of system design interviews.

So in a typical system design interview, you will be asked a specific design question eg.,(Design whatsapp, Design a search engine like google etc.) and you would have about 45 min to 1hr to come up with a system design solution with reasonable tradeoffs.

You can think of a system design round as an opportunity to work with your interviewer as a team member to solve a complex problem. It's like an open-ended brainstorming session where you have to ask a lot of questions, explore various directions of the problem and come up with the best solution within given constraints.

Now, the interviewer might even focus on specific topics out of your design to evaluate your decision making and knowledge.

One key expectation for a system design interview is that **YOU NEED TO DRIVE THE DISCUSSION** rather than the interviewer driving it.

Some of the things to keep in mind:

1. Like Data structures or algorithm questions, **there is no single solution for system design and no solution is perfect**. There can be multiple design approaches for the same problem. The main thing to focus on is to give good high-level design and discuss possible trade offs for each design and provide alternative approaches best suited for the specific problem at hand.
2. Because of the complexity of system design, it's impossible to cover all the topics and tradeoffs in one hour of interview time. So plan accordingly.

So in order to crack a system design interview, you must have a clear understanding of

1. How real world systems work and interact end to end.
2. What are the components that you need to use for instance, what kind of storage, what are apis etc. that you need to use to solve a specific problem at hand.
3. How can you actually scale the system for the next generation?

These are some of the things you should seriously focus on during your preparation.

Alright, at this point of time, I know you feel system design interviews are very daunting. However if you understand certain core concepts and follow the magical template, you should be able to approach any system interview question with great confidence.

In the next section, we will discuss a magic approach to tackle most of the system design interview questions. So let's jump into it.

The magic solution template for system design interview

Now that you know what a system design interview is, it's time to dive deep into the process of how you can actually approach and solve any kind of system design interview !

After hiring a lot of top candidates in the past and with our research on various system design resources, I have finalized a 4 step solution template to tackle any kind of system design interview.

It's called the "**READ**" technique.

READ technique to answer system design questions

READ can be described in 4 simple steps. (Underlined letters correlate to individual letters in READ)

Step 1: Requirement Analysis & Clarifications

Step 2: Estimations (Capacity estimations)

Step 3: API & Model Design

Step 4: Design & Scalability

Note that other than Step 1, you change the order of these steps as per the interviewer requirement. Try to clarify this with the interviewer that you plan to provide a solution in this high level approach and adjust according to the situation.

Alright, Let's look at each of them in detail.

Step 1: Requirement Analysis & Clarifications

System design questions are very vague.

For eg: Design a website like youtube.

When you are asked something like that, it's very important to settle down on specific requirements about the question asked with your interviewer.

1. You need to ask follow up questions, clarifications, discuss with the interviewer on what are the possible goals and scenarios and finally settle down on specific requirements of the given question.

   You should finalize on what are the inputs and outputs of the system

2. You should clearly state your assumptions that are in scope and out of scope to bring you and interviewer on the same page

So a typical requirement analysis should include

1. Functional Requirements like
   - What are the system use cases (eg: In youtube case, users should be able to upload videos, view videos, home page feed etc).
   - Who are the target users etc. (Eg: App based, browser based etc.)
2. Non functional requirements like
   - What are the expected requests per second? (Eg: How many people can view the videos simultaneously, how many videos can be uploaded in a minute etc.)

- What is the expected read to write ratio etc.(In youtube case it can be 70% reads and 30% writes)

Try to communicate and set the scope of the requirements as much as possible so that it helps you to focus on core problem solving down the line.

Let's look at an example:

Question: Design a video service like Youtube.

The possible requirements for this question can be

Functional Requirements:

1. Our system should be able to provide UI to view/stream a video for a given url like youtube.com/v1234
2. Users should be able to upload videos to make them available for others.
3. Users should be able to like or dislike a video.
4. Users should be able to make comments on videos.

Non Functional Requirements:

1. System should support parallel video views for about 30 billion views per month.
2. Video stream latency should be less than a few milliseconds.
3. System should be highly available for viewing videos.

Step 2: Estimations (Capacity estimations)

Once you settle down on certain requirements, then it's time to do some rough estimates on what kind of system you are designing.

Capacity estimates help you decide what is the scale of the system that you are trying to build. This lays foundation to some of the questions like

1. What kind of Database to choose for eg: SQL/NoSQL.
2. Should we have a caching layer?
3. Should we have a queuing system etc.

Some of the important estimation metrics that you can roughly estimate are

1. What is the Query per second (QPS) sometimes called Requests per second(RPS) the system is supposed to handle?
2. What is the storage estimate that you need to plan ahead as your system grows ?

Above are the important 2 things that will really help you understand the system complexity and scale the interviewer is expecting. Depending on the type of problem there could be other metrics that you might have to measure. **But make sure you don't spend too much time digging into calculations. Because time is key! Remember you just have 1hr.**

QPS and Storage should be good starting points for the rest of the interview.

* *Quick tip: The trick for solving Capacity estimation calculations faster is to do APPROXIMATION. Try to approximate the*

calculations as much as possible to the nearest rounded numbers (eg: 115reqs/day = approximately ~100reqs/day). In this way all the calculations can be done easily.

- Note that the interviewer is not looking for exact numbers, instead he wants to get an eye on how you approach system capacity estimations which are very common in real world day to day software jobs.
- I have compiled a list of finger tips in a cheat sheet that can be handy to solve capacity estimations in the last part of this book chapter: **Cheat Sheet for Rough Capacity Estimations.** Updated version of this cheat sheet can be found at https://pramod.me/. Basic version can be found at the end of this book as well.
- As part of Capacity estimations try to make a comment on what kind of database you might use for eg: SQL/NoSQL.

* *Quick tip: If you already know the QPS(or requests per second) and Storage estimations as part of Non-Functional requirements you might even skip the Capacity estimations step to save some time and spend the remaining interview time with the rest of the steps.*

Let's look at an example:

Question: Design a video service like Youtube.

One capacity estimation for the above question can be to calculate how many requests per second for video service.

1. Requests Per second:
    - Reads(Video views) : 30 billion/month = 1B/day = ~10K Reqs/sec

Step 3: API & Model design

The next step that you should discuss with the interviewer is the API and model design for our system.

API Design

- For each of the functional requirements that we finalized in step 1, try to have a formal API representation which helps in setting the precise stage for architecture design.
- Specify the protocol that you are going to use like HTTP/TCP etc., depending on the type of question asked.
- Mention the data exchange format that the APIs will follow for eg: JSON, XML etc.
- You can represent your APIs as REST format or Code signature format depending on your level of convenience.

Let's look at an example:

Question: Design a video service like Youtube.

The API design for youtube like service can be :

viewVideo(String videoId) : Video object

uploadVideo(User user, Video video)

likeVideo(User uer, String videoId)

dislikeVideo(User uer, String videoId)

Above representation is a kind of method signature format. You can call it out to the interviewer. If the interviewer specifically asks for REST API format, make sure you represent the API in REST format for example:

View Video

- Endpoint: GET/videos/{videoId}
- Description: Retrieve details about a specific video.
- Parameters:
    - videoId (Path Parameter): The unique identifier for the video.
- Response:
    - Returns a JSON representation of the Video object.

Upload Video

- Endpoint: POST/videos/upload
- Description: Upload a new video to the platform.
- Parameters:
    - user (Request Body): The details of the user uploading the video.
    - video (Request Body): The details of the video being uploaded.
- Response:
    - Returns a JSON representation of the uploaded Video object.

Like Video

- Endpoint: POST/videos/like/{videoId}
- Description: Add a like to a specific video.
- Parameters:
    - user (Request Body): The details of the user liking the video.

    - videoId (Path Parameter): The unique identifier for the video.
- Response:
    - Returns a confirmation message or the updated Video object.

Dislike Video

- Endpoint: POST/videos/dislike/{videoId}
- Description: Add a dislike to a specific video.
- Parameters:
    - user (Request Body): The details of the user disliking the video.
    - videoId (Path Parameter): The unique identifier for the video.
- Response:
    - Returns a confirmation message or the updated Video object.

Model Design

At this point, you have some clarity on what kind of Database you are going to use depending on capacity estimations (we will go in detail in the must learn interview questions in the upcoming chapters). Also based on rough API design, you know what kind of data objects are required to be stored and passed across the service.

So define the data model on how you plan to store the data in the respective chosen database like SQL or NoSQL.

* *Quick tip: During the interview, the sooner you define a DB schema the better it is to help understand the data flow among various components. This can later guide towards data partitioning, Relationship mapping etc.*

Let's look at an example:

Question: Design a video service like Youtube.

Model design can be :

User Table

Columns:

- user_id (Primary Key)
- username
- email
- passwordHash
- Other user-related fields (e.g., name, profile picture, etc.)

Video Table

Columns:

- video_id (Primary Key)
- title
- description
- url (assuming the video is hosted externally)
- user_id (Foreign Key referencing user_id in the User Table)
- Other video-related fields (e.g., upload date, duration, etc.)

Like Table

Columns:

- like_id (Primary Key)
- user_id (Foreign Key referencing user_id in the User Table)
- video_id (Foreign Key referencing video_id in the Video Table)

Dislike Table

Columns:

- dislike_id (Primary Key)
- user_id (Foreign Key referencing user_id in the User Table)
- video_id (Foreign Key referencing video_id in the Video Table)

This schema represents a rough structure for the functionalities. Each table has a primary key, and relationships between tables are established using foreign keys. The Video table is associated with the User table to keep track of the user who uploaded each video. The Like and Dislike tables are used to record user interactions with videos. Feel free to experiment with your own database schema design.

Step 4: Design and Scalability

Next comes the most important part of the interview. Until this step we have just laid a structure of what are overall requirements, capacity estimations and data model. Now it's time to connect the pieces and discuss the end to end flow for the whole system. So in this step,

- Draw high level diagrams of what kind of components needs to be present in the system. What services need to be used.
- Connect each of these components with arrows to represent the read and write flows and how the data is transported end to end in each of the flows.
- Typical components can include app servers, load balancers, database, cache servers, queueing systems, custom metric systems etc.
- Once you discuss on a high level, then do a deep dive with each of the components on what are the possible problems for your solution and discuss various approaches to solve the specific workflow.
- During the dive deep you should focus on how you will scale the application further and what new components you need to develop or integrate.
- Make sure you cover all the workflows for the APIs that you defined previously by making respective connections.
- Talk about the problems, tradeoffs you make and how you scale the system for multiple workloads.
- Try to identify bottlenecks and address the same for each of the components you are trying to build.

* ***Note: Keep in mind that some interviewers might ask to start with High level design even before the Capacity estimations step or API design step. So communicate this with your interviewer and adjust the steps as per interviewer preference.***

This section is the main area where most of the interview time is spent.

Let's look at an example:

Question: Design a video service like Youtube.

Basic high level design for youtube like video service can be as shown in the below diagram.

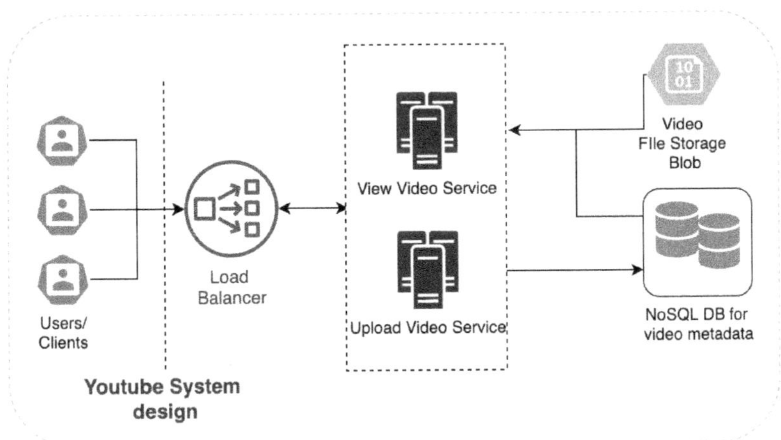

Basic system design for Youtube like service

Above diagram can be a good start point for youtube service. From here you can discuss various approaches by diving deep into concepts like compressing video, encoding /decoding video formats, cache, queues and introducing or modifying new components accordingly.

Once the interviewer is ok, you can share some final thoughts about the final system you designed and how you can further scale to the future.

- At this step discuss different metrics about the system and how you can enhance it further.
- How you expand your system to different geographical locations using CDNs.

- Discuss about how you can onboard future requirements.
- Mostly at this point your interviewer would ask further questions and the discussion can go accordingly.

Let's look at an example:

Question: Design a video service like Youtube.

In the YouTube case, you can talk about dividing your service further into multiple microservices. Introducing multiple load balancers between different components. You can talk about how you can further reduce video streaming latency across different geographical locations. How to track what kind of videos users are watching through metrics etc.

Alright now that you know the ***READ*** technique, in the following chapters we will first dive into individual system design topics everyone should know. Post that we will dive into must learn system design interview questions applying the READ technique to learn and crack system design interviews.

Chapter 3

System Design Basics

In this section we will discuss some of the important system design basics.

1. Lifecycle of a web request

In order to do robust system design, it's very important to understand how systems interact end to end. In this section, we will discuss the high level lifecycle of a real world web application request.

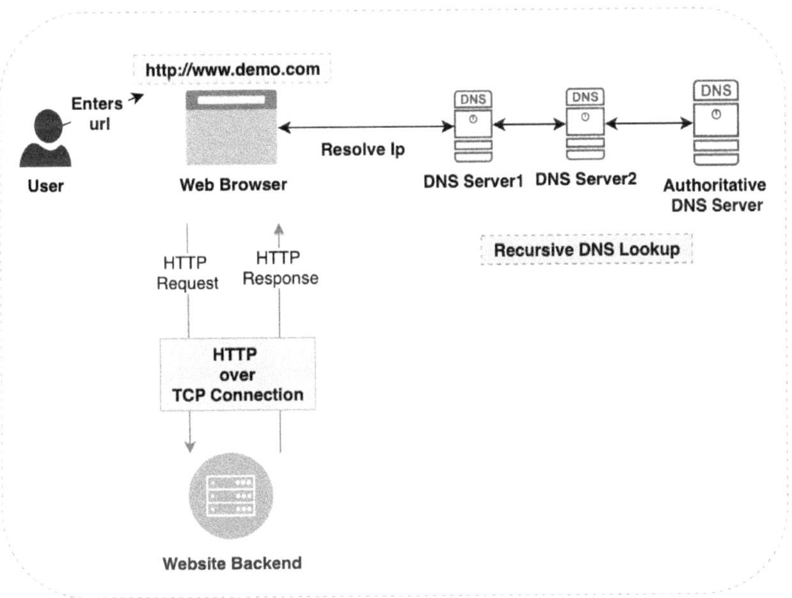

Lifecycle of a web request

The primary goal of a typical web application is to take incoming user requests, do some work and return the response to the user.

In between user request and server response there is a lot of process that happens. Let's look at a sample request.

Let's say a user tries to access a website with a url : www.tipseason.com. A user enters a url on a web browser either in laptop/computer/mobile devices/some programmatic terminal. For simplicity let's assume a web browser.

- First thing browser does is to parse the url into various details as per the below syntax
- <protocol>://<host><:optional port>/<path/to/resource><?queryParams>. An example :
- http://www.tipseason.com:8000/home?user=pramod
- is parsed into
- |http|://|www.tipseason.com||:8000||/home||?user=pramod|
- Next thing the browser does is to find a path to connect to the domain of the website url that is entered. In order to connect to a specific domain, its respective ip address needs to be resolved.
- Just the way we have our own phone number, every website has an assigned ip address that clients can connect to. Ip address lays a routing path over the internet. Since it's easy to remember a name rather than ip addresses, domain names have been introduced. So every website domain is nothing but a name for an ip address. These ip to domain name mapping records are called domain name server (DNS) records. DNS record is a Domain Name Server record

which is nothing but the ip address of the url domain that is entered. Every domain resolves to a specific ip address for eg: www.google.com can have an ip like 172.217.164.110. So if you'd like to reach www.google.com you can even type http://172.217.164.110:80, where 80 is the port to connect on your browser.

- So the Browser takes the domain part of the url and checks for DNS records of the host. It first checks in local cache for the DNS record, if it doesn't exist it checks for records in a DNS server recursively across multiple available DNS servers based on network and internet provider configurations.
- Once the DNS records are resolved to an ip address, the browser initiates a TCP connection with the target server behind the ip. Now that connection is established between the client and the server, user data is sent in the form of HTTP Request via the established TCP connection.
- HTTP Request consists of header part and Body part.
- This request is sent to the server
- Server takes the request and performs the appropriate action and returns the response back to the client via the same tcp connection.

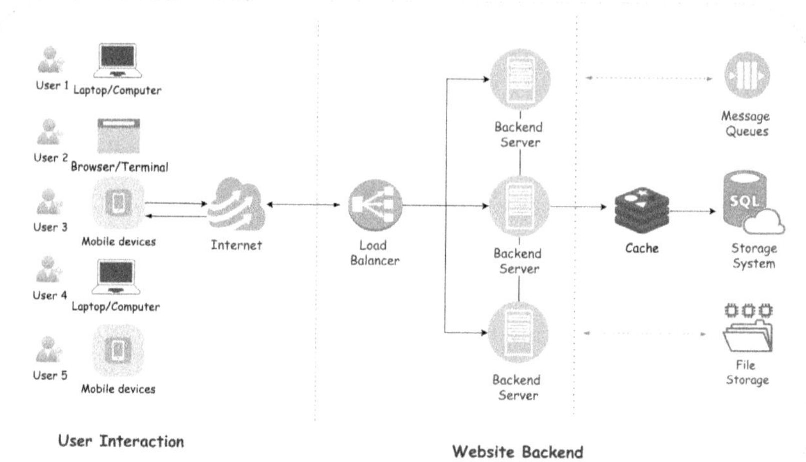

System design for real world large scale applications

Users can connect to our website with a computer, laptop, mobile browser or mobile apps. Let's say a user entered a url (http://www.google.com) in a web browser. Once the user tries to access a specific url (say: www.hello.com), the request is sent over the internet as shown in the image above. This request is handled by the load balancer for our website backend. Load balancer is a component which distributes load to multiple servers for processing the requests. So the request is taken by one of the backend servers i.e. the app servers to process the respective action based on the request. Backend servers can communicate with different application level components like Cache, Distributed message queues, SQL or NoSQL storage systems, File storage systems etc. After reaching out to multiple components, backend servers can send a response to the incoming client which is connected via the load balancer. We will learn more about each of these components in the "System Design Basics" section.

System design is all about how we can interact with each of the components to provide an efficient response to the incoming clients based on the type of application. We have seen that each of the components interact with each other. In order to have the interaction there should be some kind of unified message format which can be used across each of the layers. JSON (JavaScript Object Notation) or XML (Extensible Markup Language) are some of the popular message exchange format schemes with which data can be sent over the wire.

In most web applications these requests are sent using HTTP protocol over a TCP connection. For some of the applications like video buffering, real time audio streaming etc uses UDP for communication. We will learn more about these in the next section.

TCP Vs UDP Protocols

TCP and UDP are one of the core protocols for the transport layer of communication.

Some applications require TCP connections while some other applications require UDP. Let's look at each of them.

TCP

TCP (Transmission control protocol) is a connection oriented protocol. What it means is that if we have to exchange data between two parties, say a client (party which receives the data) and server(sender of data) both the parties should be connected to each other. A client initiates a connection with the server and a session is maintained between both of them within which the subsequent communication happens. Connection establishment is a very humble three step process. First the client sends a SYN packet to the server. Server checks it and gives an acknowledgement to the client saying SYN-ACK. Finally the client sends back a ACK packet back to the server with the sequence number and the whole connection is established. This process is called the *three way handshake mechanism.* Once the connection is established the communication data bytes can flow through this TCP connection.

Similar to connection establishment, connection termination also follows multiple steps with the FIN, ACK packets.

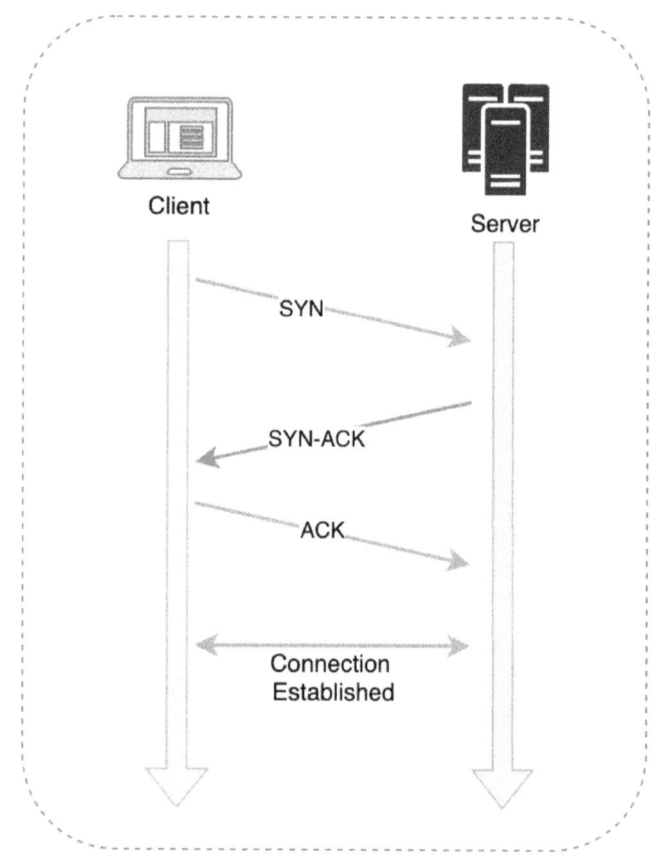

TCP Connection Establishment Timeline

TCP guarantees message ordering, retransmission of lost packets, error free data transfer etc. Most web applications use TCP for communication because it is a reliable way to exchange the communication between the applications.

UDP

UDP (User datagram protocol) is a connectionless protocol. Connectionless protocols do not set up a dedicated end-to-end connection. Communication is achieved by transmitting information in one direction from source to destination without verifying the readiness or state of the receiver. With a simple transmission method without implied hand-shaking dialogues for ordering, reliability, or data integrity UDP can be called as a message oriented protocol. An application binds a socket to its endpoint of data transmission, which is a combination of an IP address and a port. Message ordering, error correction is not possible with UDP.

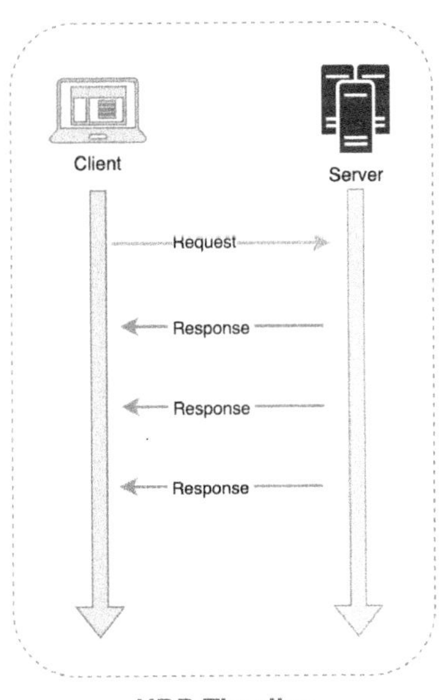

UDP Timeline

In a typical UDP connection client Requests the server for data. Server can send multiple response packets as shown in the above diagram. Video streaming, real time audio streaming are some good examples which use UDP for communication because it's ok to have occasional packet loss during message transmission for video buffering.

2. Distributed Systems Core Concepts

When designing any large scale distributed system, some of the important factors we need to keep in mind are as follows.

2.1 Scalability

All big things start with small beginnings.

Every application starts with a small setup in the beginning. Probably with a server, database etc. Initially as the number of users are less there may not be bigger problems. But as the number of users grows, applications should be able to support the increased requests and complex workload. This process of making the system adjust according to the increased or decreased workload is called System Scalability.

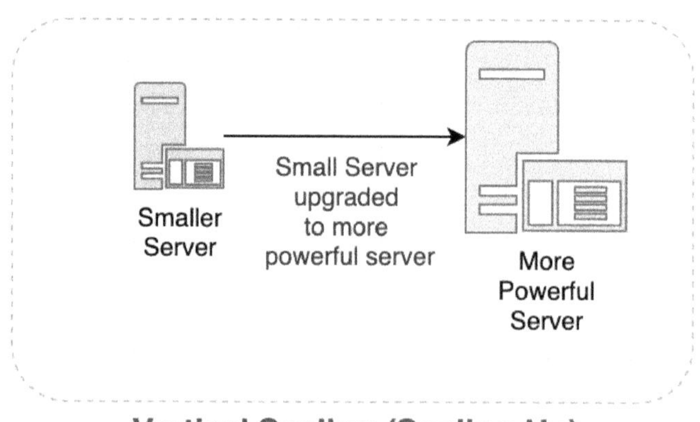

Vertical Scaling (Scaling Up)

Vertical Scaling (Scaling Up)

Let's say we started our website with a single app server and a database, and the user base is slowly growing up. As the number of users grow, in order for the system to be scalable one way to increase the overall processing capacity is to upgrade the physical hardware like increased RAM, increased CPU, HDD etc. This way of scaling the system by increasing more infrastructure is called Vertical Scaling i.e.,Scaling Up.

The advantage of vertical scaling is that if we have good hardware at hand, replacing powerful hardware can definitely increase processing capacity in faster time without changing the overall system complexity.

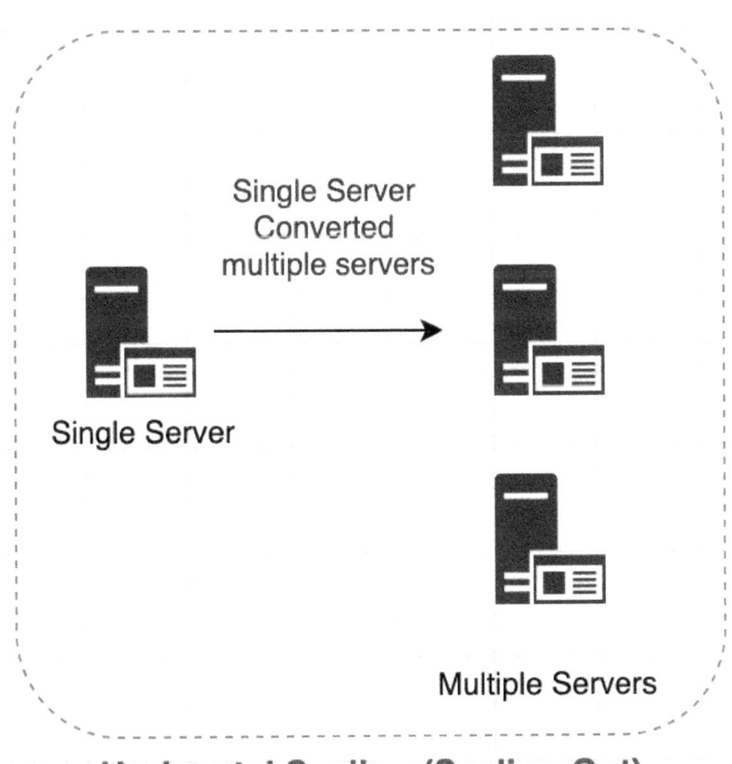

Horizontal Scaling (Scaling Out)

Horizontal Scaling (Scaling Out)

Increasing the system hardware to achieve scalability can be good for a limited time or for some specific applications. But the capacity of hardware is limited and if the traffic demand is beyond the hardware capacity, then it's time to have multiple resources instead of a single resource doing the whole job. Horizontal scaling (also called as Scaling Out) means adding multiple resources to an existing pool. We can add multiple app servers instead of having one, multiple database servers, multiple cache servers, multiple queueing systems etc. Since we increase multiple resources for various components, we should also have a distribution and coordination mechanism to make these components work together. So horizontal scaling involves more complexity than vertical scaling.

Horizontal scaling scales pretty well for increased system load. Some Comparison Points:

- In horizontal scaling, since there are multiple resources for the same task, we can avoid the single point of failure compared to vertical scaling.
- Since multiple resources are involved in horizontal scaling, it's important to maintain data consistency across the servers.
- In horizontal scaling we would need a load balancer to distribute load across resources.

2.2 High Availability & Reliability

High availability(HA) is when our application is always up and running without any interruption. It's the ability to serve the users without much downtime even during system updates. A typical 99.9% system availability implies the system is up and running with only a scope of 8.77 hours per year of downtime. 99.99% implies the system can be down only for 52.6 minutes per year. In order to have high availability, we should optimize each component by handling failure handling, scalability, data replication etc.

Reliability is often related to High Availability. High availability is the probability that the system is operating properly *when it is requested for use.* Reliability represents the probability of components, parts and systems to perform their required functions *for a desired period of time.* In distributed systems, both these factors play a key role.

2.3 Fault Tolerance

Distributed systems involve multiple resources of various components. Any of the system resources can fail at a given point. For example an app server can go down due to out of memory, a database server can go down due to hard disk failure. A cache cluster can go inaccessible due to network partition and so on. Fault tolerance is the ability of the system to recover from failures. When we design any system, we should always have a question in mind : What happens if a specific resource goes down? We might have to introduce fallback systems or add redundant resources etc. Preparing for failures is what fault tolerance leads to. Every distributed system should be fault tolerant in order to serve continuously.

Resilience Patterns

Fault tolerance and Fault resilience are sometimes used interchangeably. Basically fault tolerance indicates the ability of the system to recover from failures.

Fault Tolerance: means that any user of the service exported from the cluster does not observe any fault (other than possibly a longer delay than is normal) during a fallback mechanism.

Fault Resilience: means that a fault may be observed, but only in uncommitted data (i.e. the database may respond with an error to the attempt to commit a transaction, etc.). Most commonly used resilience patterns are as below.

Pattern	How it works
Rate Limiter	It limits the number of executions that can happen in a certain time. Limits the rate of incoming requests to a specific service. There can be various types like static rate limiter, rolling rate limiter etc.
Retry	This is the most commonly used mechanism if some failure occurs. It makes the system retry the request if a specific resource fails
Circuit Breaker	When a system is seriously struggling, it's better to return fast failure responses to the clients rather than making the clients wait for a long time. In that way the caller can do a fallback mechanism. Circuit breaker temporarily blocks possible failures.
Time Limiter	Setting up a time limit on how much time a request can wait. Typically these are the system timeouts.

Pattern	How it works
Fallback	When some failure occurs it's better to fail over to a secondary resource that is backed up to the primary resource.
Bulkhead	Resources are grouped into pools and isolated from each other so that even if one pool is failing another pool can continue to work.

Reference: https://github.com/resilience4j/resilience4j#overview

2.4 Performance

Performance of a system is how fast a response can be made to a given request. Latency is the amount of time it takes to do some work. High performance systems have very low latency and high throughput(Number of processed requests in a given amount of time). Needless to say, if we want our users to keep using our system, our system should serve the requests fast enough with efficiency.

3. Load Balancer

Most modern applications require multiple app servers to process incoming requests. In order to distribute the traffic across these servers, there should be some component that can take the incoming requests and route the traffic uniformly. Load balancer is the exact component which does the balancing functionality.

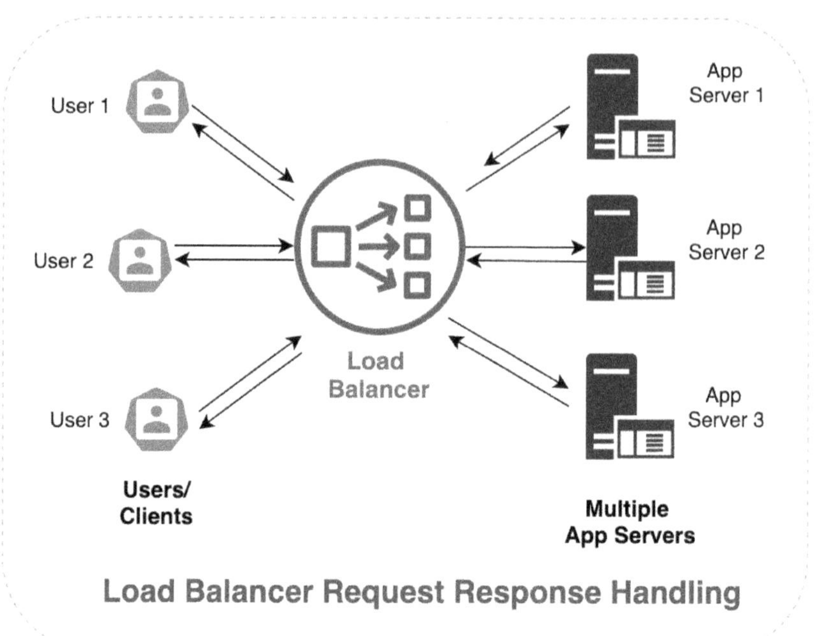

- As shown in the image above, if a user tries to send a request to the application, it is sent to the load balancer first. Load balancer chooses the destination server with least load (based on the routing algorithms discussed in the following section) and sends the traffic to the specific app server. Once the app server handles the request, it sends the response back to the load balancer which in turn sends the data back to the user. (Follow the User2 arrows in above diagram)
- If multiple users try to connect to the website, the load balancer takes all the incoming user requests and distributes the load uniformly across multiple servers
- In addition to user facing load balancers, there could be server to server and server to database load balancers that can do internal routing.

- During the process of handling requests, load balancers also keep track of how many servers are online and offline at a given instance and distribute the traffic only to online servers. In this way a single point of failure can be avoided and adding/modifying servers can be done easily.

So overall load balancer helps in horizontal scaling of the system to handle increased load.

Hardware Vs Software Load Balancer

Load balancer can be implemented at a Software level or Hardware level.

- **Hardware Load balancer:** Hardware load balancers rely on specific hardware devices specially designed to do load distribution. The advantage of a hardware load balancer is the better performance compared to software one. The disadvantage is the physical equipment provisioning time and cost.
- **Software Load balancer:** Software load balancer is typically a software installed on a server or group of servers. The advantage of software vs hardware one is that it's more scalable and cost effective compared to hardware ones. The disadvantage is the performance degradation compared to hardware load balancers.

Load Balancer Types

Based on the level at which load balancer can be applied, they can be of different types.

1. **Application Load Balancer:** Makes routing based on application layer (L7 of OSI model) i.e. HTTP/HTTPS. Some parameters for this could be like HTTP header, uniform

resource identifier, SSL session ID and HTML form data. This is one of the most useful forms especially for microservice load balancing by urls.

2. **Network Load Balancer:** Acts at L4 Layer of OSI model. It directs traffic based on data from network and transport layer protocols such as TCP/UDP traffic. Network load balancing is considered the fastest of all the load balancing solutions, but it tends to fall short when it comes to balancing the distribution of traffic across multiple servers.
3. **Global Server Load Balancing(GSLB):** Global Server Load Balancing is an extended version of L4 and L7 capabilities to servers in different geographic locations.

Load Balancer Routing Algorithms

The routing logic (i.e. *How does load balancer pick a specific server for traffic distribution*) for load balancers can be configured with various techniques. Based on the type of application, one of the below routing algorithms can be chosen to do the routing

- **Round Robin Method:** In this method, load balancer sends the requests to each of the servers sequentially in a cycle irrespective of processing time. So when the current server is the last server, the next request goes to the first server. If most requests take similar time and that all servers have equal configuration, this method has more advantage. If not it can create bottlenecks to few servers as specific servers can be overloaded due to unequal processing times.
- **Least Connection Method:** In this method, load balancer will keep track of how many connections are active for each of the servers and pick the one that has least active connections.

- **Least Response Time Method:** This is a combination of Least Connection Method + Least client response time. So a server which has the least connections and which can give a response in the least time is chosen as the next server.
- **Least Bandwidth Method:** This method is mostly applied to bandwidth intensive applications for example, video upload etc. Here the server with least bandwidth utilization is chosen as the next server.
- **Hash Methods:** Hash methods such as URL Hash or IP Hash are one of the popular methods. In this method, a hash value is generated with request url or the client IP address as key. Based on the hash value, a specific target server is chosen. Some of the load balancers support Consistent Hashing for effective load balancing. Details of Consistent Hashing are discussed in a separate section.
- **Weighted Round Robin Method:** This is an extension to the round robin method. Instead of doing cycles, each server is given a weight based on the processing capacity. Server with the highest weight receives new and more connections before those with less weights.

Load Balancer Scalability

Load balancers themselves need to be scalable since they are the primary request routing servers. So they tend to be a single point of failure if not configured properly. To avoid that, we can have a secondary load balancer setup which can take over as master based on the health of the primary load balancer.

In a nutshell load balancer can be configured either in Active-Passive(primary and secondary load balancer setup) or Active-Active mode (Multiple server sharing load distribution).

Extra Reads

https://lethain.com/introduction-to-architecting-systems-for-scale/

https://www.nginx.com/resources/glossary/load-balancing/

https://avinetworks.com/what-is-load-balancing/

4. Caching

As the applications grow bigger, it's important to provide faster access to underlying data. Cache can be referred to as a high speed data storage layer, which stores a subset of actual data so that repeated requests to the same subset of data can have faster access than with the persistent storage.

- A **cache hit** occurs when the requested data can be found in a cache, while a **cache miss** occurs when it cannot.
- Traditional database systems store data in a disk for persistent storage. Reading data from disk involves physical rotation of the disk to seek specific addresses of data. Since this involves physical movement, speed is limited by how fast the disk can rotate to access a specific location. So data access is slower. In order to avoid these slow reads, all the frequently accessed data can be stored in memory i.e., RAM so that speed is driven by fastness of digital data movement. This way of speeding up the reads can be called Caching.
- Another way to speed up the data is to have the data closer to the processing system. The CPU uses L1,L2, L3 etc. level cache which is the closest storage for faster processing.
- Cache storage is mostly temporary in nature like RAM. But sometimes, cache can be persistent too. For example web

browsers cache frequently accessed images and flash in local hard disk instead of fetching freshly from the internet every time. This is also a type of caching pattern. The goal is to get faster access to data without querying the primary source.

Cache can be at all levels of computing like web applications, operating systems, hardware, web browsers etc. In distributed systems cases, cache between user facing servers and databases is one of the most commonly used cache.

Let's look at a few caching levels.

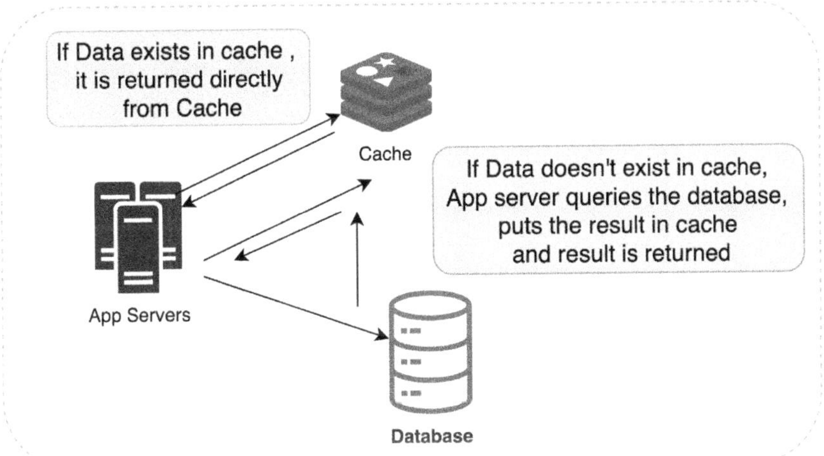

Application Layer Cache

Application level caching involves app level code or library which does the cache management. In this type, app servers first try to get the data from the cache layer. If the data is not present in cache it fetches the data from the database, puts it into cache and then returns the data to the request. In this way all the future requests of the same data are fetched directly from the cache. So for application level caching there can be a dedicated caching framework like redis or memcached for caching layer.

In-Memory Cache

Having a dedicated cache storage itself can sometimes be slower as it can involve data transfer over the wire. For very small data, we can use app server memory itself for caching the data. Data Structures like HashMap can be used for O(1) lookups for app server level in memory caching. Some of the external libraries like Google Guava support in memory caching via `CacheBuilder` library code.

Content Delivery Network (CDN)

In large scale applications, data might be stored across different geographical locations. So data requests can take longer if they have to travel to different regions. A CDN(Content Delivery Network) is most useful to cache static website content like images, videos, webpages etc. A CDN caches static content in proxy servers that are located closer to end users. If a specific resource is not located in the nearest server, a CDN queries the source server, caches the data in the local server and serves the content to the user. In this way future requests to that data file can be faster.

How to invalidate the cache data?

Whenever the data is modified in the persistent storage, it should be reflected even in the cache data, or else there is a chance to return wrong data to the requests. In order to do this, the following methods can be used.

1. **Write Around Cache:** In this process, the data is written directly to the database and the cache data is marked as invalid. Due to this, the request to cache data is considered as cache miss and is forced to reload the data from DB and

put it in cache. This is one of the most commonly used cache invalidation methods.

2. **Write Through Cache:** In this process, the data is written both to the cache as well as the database. Since this method involves writing the data in both the cache and database, the latency of write requests can be higher. However, read requests will reflect the latest data faster with minimal latency.
3. **Write Back Cache:** In this process data is written only to the Cache layer. There can be a background process which can periodically fetch the data from cache and put it in persistent storage. The disadvantage with this method is the data loss since the server can cache in between the fetch intervals.

If we are dealing with a single data center then cache invalidation is relatively easier than when dealing with multiple datacenters as the data updated needs to be persisted across data centers and cache invalidations should happen in parallel.

Cache data eviction

In most caches, we saw that in case of cache miss the data is fetched from the database and put it into cache and data is returned. But we know that cache memory is limited in size and more expensive. So we need to have some kind of way to remove unwanted data from cache which is called cache eviction. There are few ways to do data eviction

- Least Recently Used (LRU) Cache: LRU is one of the most used caching mechanisms. In this mechanism if the cache size is full, the data that is not accessed recently is removed first, so that the most recent data can be inserted. Cache insertion time is the main factor for eviction.

- Least Frequently Used (LFU) Cache : In case of LFU cache, the data that is least frequently used is removed first to provide space for new inserts. So everytime a cache hit is made, it increments the counter for that key. If the cache is full, the key with least count is removed first.
- Most Recently Used (MRU) Cache: This is opposite to the LRU cache. Data that is most recently used is removed first. One sample use case of MRU is a video media player. The video that is most recently played has the least chance of watching it again compared to fresh ones.
- First In First Out (FIFO) Cache: In this, the data that came into the cache first is removed first. Think of it like a queue model. Irrespective of when the data is accessed recently or not data is evicted whichever comes first into cache.
- Last In First Out (LIFO) Cache: In this cache, the data that came in last will be removed first. This is like the Stack model. Irrespective of how frequently or recently the data is accessed, data which came in last will be removed first.
- Random Replacement(RR) Cache: In this type, data is replaced randomly from cache.

Practical Caching Frameworks:

Some of the widely used distributed caching frameworks are Redis(https://redis.io/), Memcache etc. Both of these store data in memory. Redis is the most popular caching framework as it supports multiple data structures within the cached data. Lot of components are built on top of redis. Redis provides data structures such as strings, hashes, lists, sets, sorted sets with range queries, bitmaps, hyperloglogs, geospatial indexes, and streams. Redis has a built-in replication and scripting framework based out of Lua. I would strongly recommend experimenting with Redis.

5. Queues

Before jumping into Queues, let's understand what is Online processing (Synchronous processing) and Offline processing (Asynchronous processing). Let's say a user is trying to do a twitter post. The primary task involved for a post is to save the tweet data in db right. But in addition to that there can be some secondary tasks like sending notifications to the intended recipient, collecting tweet metrics, distributing tweets to various user timelines and so on. So if we do all the above operations in the user request itself then the person doing a tweet should wait for a long time until all the above processes are complete to get a successful response from the server. So to have a good user experience and to have a highly scalable system, we need to offload some of the secondary tasks away from user request threads. This process of performing secondary tasks independent of the main request thread without having to wait is called offline processing (Asynchronous processing). Whatever the primary task (in this case saving to db) that keeps the request waiting is called 'Online processing (Synchronous processing)'. Online tasks and offline tasks need not be just in the context of user request threads, instead they can be in backend process handling too.

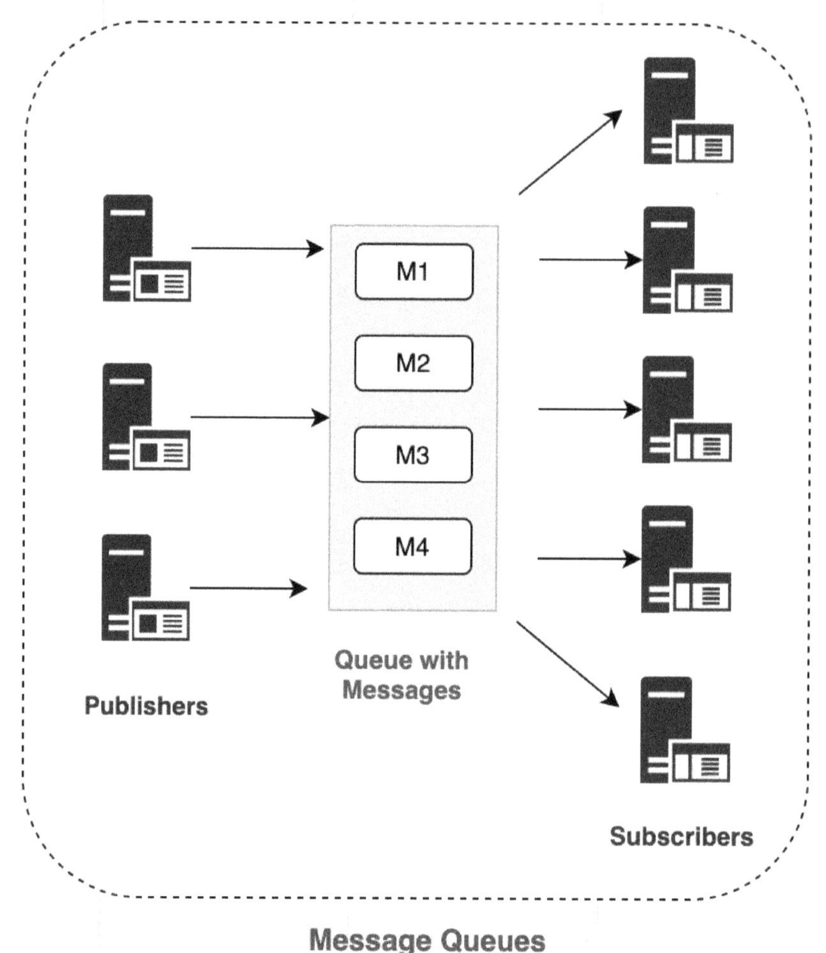

Message Queues

So in the above example, if we have to achieve asynchronous handling, the data needs to be passed between the publishers (the caller) and subscribers (the processing threads). Queues come into picture at this level. Message queues let the publishers save the data in them. Subscribers listen to message queues for new messages and process each of the messages. There could be multiple subscribers to the same queue. Similarly there could be multiple publishers to the message queue. Having this kind of system enables the caller to execute primary tasks and publish the message to the message queue and return the result back to the caller immediately. Later on subscribers can execute secondary tasks by listening to queues. Message queues can be in memory or persistent. Distributed message queues enable the application to have distributed processing across multiple workloads.

Some of the most widely used distributed message queues are Kafka, RabbitMQ, AWS SQS, Azure service bus etc.

For system design interviews, message queues play a major role for offloading tasks. As part of your scalability design make sure you have discussions about queueing with your interviewer. Also before going to an interview, try to play around with at least one distributed queue if not already.

6. Polling, Long Polling, Web sockets, Server send events

Communication between a client and a server requires some kind of protocol in which the connection is established, data is exchanged. Among the two most common transport protocols TCP and UDP, TCP is reliable and UDP isn't. HTTP is a widely used protocol that relies on TCP which is connection based for reliable communication. Let's look at how HTTP works.

- A client which needs to perform some action, establishes a connection with the server.
- Client sends data as per the HTTP Request message format (https://www.w3.org/Protocols/rfc2616/rfc2616-sec4.html) to the server as part of the connection that is established.

- Server reads the http request message and performs the appropriate action and sends the data back as per the HTTP Response format to the client in the same connection.
- Connection is closed once the exchange is complete.

Now that we know how HTTP works, let's look at more communication patterns between server and client.

To understand the communication patterns let's take an example of 'Notifications'. We receive a lot of notifications every day like a New Chat notification, New Email arrival, New Tweet notifications, new facebook post notifications etc., right. If we have to implement this kind of communication we can do it in two ways.

1. **Pull Model:** In a pull model, a client asks the server periodically to see if any data has changed. Polling is an example for this.
2. **Push Model:** In a push model, the server sends data to the client if any new data has changed. Connection establishment in the case of push models can be tricky compared to pull models.

Let's look at various techniques:

Pull Model Techniques

Polling

Polling is a technique where a client asks the server periodically to see if any new data has come.

- Clients can make a http connection every few seconds (or some configured time) to receive response from the server. If new data exists, the server returns that data as part of the response. Else it can return an empty response.

- For instance in a new chat message notification case, the client can make a Http connection with the server periodically to see if there are any new emails that came.
- The connection with the server is closed immediately once the response is received.
- Since polling involves frequent requests with a server, there could be more latency for connection establishment, processing and response. This may not be scalable as the system grows.

Long Polling

Long polling is an improved version of polling. In case of long polling

- Once a client establishes a connection with the server, it sends a request for any new data changes. This connection is kept open until a certain timeout has reached or if some data change response is available.
- If the server has some change in data, it can send a response back to the client as part of the open connection itself.
- Once the response is received the client can read the response and reinitiate a fresh connection request.
- In this way, the problem of frequent connections in polling can be reduced to a wide extent.
- Long polling is still a unidirectional technique as it's based on HTTP i.e., client sends request and server sends the response. There is no way a server can send a response without a client request.

Push Model Techniques

Server Sent Events (SSEs)

Since polling involves continuous connection establishment, Server sent events(SSE) can be used to achieve a push mechanism for new changes.

- In SSE, the client establishes a connection with the server. It sends a HTTP Request to the server and expects a response with a stream of event messages over time.
- The connection is kept open by the server and multiple responses are sent to the client until it has no more events to send. Server decides that the connection has been open long enough and can be considered stale, or until the client explicitly closes the initial request.
- SSEs are still a unidirectional system i.e., as part of the established connection, the client can send requests to the server only during the initial request. After that only the server can send responses but the client can't send requests again.
- SSEs can be widely used for single sided push applications like real time news feed, Stock price changes etc.

Web Sockets

The problem with SSEs is that it's unidirectional. Websockets solve this problem.

- Websocket provides a full duplex communication channel between server and client. Connection between server and client is persistent so that both server and client can send data at any time over the same persistent connection.

- The Connection uses the "*Connection: Upgrade*" header during connection establishment. This header gives a signal that we want to keep the connection alive, and use it for non-HTTP requests. In this way a persistent connection can be made.
- Since the connection is always open and that it's not a HTTP request, either server or client can send messages bidirectionally and at the same time.
- So in short, websockets enable bidirectional communication between server and client and provide lightweight objects for keeping the connections alive with various headers. Heartbeat can be sent across the websocket connections that will further make sure both server and client are connected to each other.
- Modern languages and clients have robust support for websockets which can be used to build applications on top of websockets.
- Chapter: "Design whatsapp messaging system" is one example of how we can efficiently use websockets for real time communication. You can refer the same for websockets usage.

Now that we know various communication patterns, during the system design interviews it's important to apply these techniques based on the type of question asked. For example, if the question is to design a Whatsapp Chat like application, then we can discuss SSEs, websockets etc. For general applications without real time communication, we can discuss HTTP and polling as required.

7. Storage systems

Average human brain memory capacity is about 2.5 Petabytes.

Everything in this world needs to be stored in some place in order to access it at a later point of time. Computing storage is no different than this.

File Storage

All the files for eg: Images, videos, documents are stored as part of a storage system in the form of files. File storage is the system of storing data in the form of files and presenting it to the user in the form of hierarchical directories (of folders) structure. Eg: "/home/pramodnanduri/images/hello.jpeg". File system controls how the data is stored and retrieved. Typically file storage is a permanent storage. Hard disks, SSDs, Optical Disks etc., are some of the examples of permanent file storage. File systems are mostly used to store unstructured data. In a file system, data can be stored in the form of small chunks called blocks. Each block can be sequential to each other or split across the storage. If we distribute these blocks across multiple machines we can call that as a Distributed file system. In a distributed file system, a large file is split into multiple smaller files and each file is split into multiple blocks of equal size (eg: 128MB blocks) and these blocks can be spread across multiple machines. Apache HDFS (Hadoop distributed file system) is one good example of distributed file systems. Distributed file systems involve quite a bit of underlying complexity to manage the files and this complexity is abstracted by these open frameworks like HDFS or Amazon S3 etc.

Databases

In file storage, all the data is stored as it is in unorganized chunks. A Database is a collection of information that is organized and structured in a specific format so that it's easy to read, write in different data queries. Database uses file storage to store the underlying data but it forms an abstraction to how this data is queried and indexed to the end user. Databases can be of two types

1. Relational Databases i.e. SQL Databases
2. Non Relational databases i.e. NoSQL Database.

Let's look at each of them.

7.1 Relational Databases (SQL Databases)

SQL Databases are also called relational databases i.e. we can define relations between various data tables and queries can be built dynamically based on the table schema and column patterns. All the data is divided in the form of Tables. Each table can have multiple Columns and Rows. In a SQL database, columns are fixed. Data can be inserted and retrieved from the tables in the form of rows. Each table column can have indexes for faster access of data. We can form joins between individual tables and query the data forming relationships across the data tables. Some of the popular SQL databases include MySQL, Microsoft SQL Server, Oracle Database, MariaDB, PostGREs etc. CRUD (Create, Read, Update, Delete) operations can be performed on the tables databases using predefined SQL query syntax. Most SQL databases rely on master-slave setup for data replication. Master server servers as the primary node for serving data. Slave server continuously syncs the data from the master server. If for some reason the master fails, the slave will take over as a master to serve the requests.

Transaction Management is one of the key features of SQL. Let's say we want to perform multiple operations on our data with multiple queries, if we want to execute multiple queries as a single unit of work i.e. either all the queries will succeed or all of them fail, this can be achieved with transactions. One example to understand is Bank account transfer. If you want to transfer money from one account to a second account, we need to debit money from the source account and credit money to the destination account. While executing these SQL operations, if there is any failure in the system or data, then the money should not be debited from the source nor credited to the destination. If at all some partial happens, it should be reverted to the previous account balances. So these two operations need to be treated as a single unit and work needs to be done. This is called transaction management. SQL databases exhibit **ACID** (Atomicity, Consistency, Isolation, Durability.) properties for transaction management. Let's look at each of them.

ACID indicates :

Atomicity: Transactions often involve multiple SQL queries. Atomicity guarantees that all the queries are executed as a single unit which either succeeds or fails completely. While executing the queries, if any of the statements fail either due to data inconsistency or system failures then the data needs to be rolled back to the cleaner state before the query execution.

Consistency: In a distributed environment, if there are multiple nodes (or machines) involved in serving the data, then every node should return the same, most recent data. Consistency ensures that the transactions can only bring the database to valid state in spite of predefined rules, constraints, cascades, triggers present in the database.

Isolation: Transactions are often executed concurrently. So each query can run in parallel for the underlying operation. Even though the transaction happens concurrently, the underlying data state should be similar to the state when the queries execute sequentially. Isolation ensures concurrency control.

Durability: Systems can fail indefinitely for eg: Power failures, Network partitions etc. Durability ensures the data is committed in spite of system failures.

Now that we have seen the advantages of our databases, it's important to scale the SQL database without compromising the above properties. Inorder to scale the databases we can do either vertical scaling by increasing database power or horizontal scaling by dividing the data. Sharding is a key technique to achieve database scaling.

Database Sharding

As the database size grows, we tend to have billions of rows in each of the SQL tables. As the number of rows grows, index size also grows. Due to this query performance is affected. Also most SQL systems rely on Master slave setup for storing the data. So having a single master to serve all the data needs may not be scalable. Sharding solves this problem. Sharding is a process of dividing the data into smaller partitions and spreading it across multiple machines for improving performance, availability. Database sharding can be achieved through various ways.

1. **Table Level Sharding:** In this form of sharding, each table is split into multiple tables based on some sharding criteria.

Rows of each table are split into multiple tables and served. In fewer cases, tables are split based on the column wise too.

2. **Schema Level Sharding:** In SQL systems, data can be stored in multiple schemas (called databases synonymously). Tables can be split across multiple schemas and each schema can be served from a different node.

These sharding schemes can be referred to as horizontal and vertical sharding. Horizontal sharding involves putting different rows in different tables and vertical sharding involves separating databases based on the type of feature for eg: In youtube system design, comments can be put in one database, video ratings can be put in a different database. Overall the main goal is to split the data based on some logical key according to the application needs and achieve reliability, performance.

7.2 NoSQL Databases (Non relational databases)

NoSQL Databases are also called non relational databases. They are different from the traditional relational databases in the way the data is stored and retrieved with flexible schemas for building most modern applications. Data is stored in a non-tabular form either as key-value pairs or in the form of documents. Let's look at the most common NoSQL storage models.

Key-Value Databases

Key value databases are the simplest of all the NoSQL databases yet more powerful. Data is stored in the form of key value pairs and can be distributed easily across various nodes separated by keys. Some of the highly used systems like Cache etc, are stored in key value pairs using NoSQL mechanism. Redis, Memcached are some of the examples of Key value databases.

Column Oriented Databases

Relational databases have fixed sets of columns. When a table schema is defined, these columns are preconfigured and data is stored in the form of rows. Each row will have these fixed sets of columns. Column oriented databases take a different approach. In these types of databases, each row can have a dynamic number of columns and columns need not be defined during the table creation. Data can grow dynamically as wide columns. HBase and Cassandra are typical examples of column oriented databases. You can think of these databases as multi dimensional map storage.

	ColumnFamily1				ColumnFamily2			
	Column1	Column2	Column3	.....	Column1	Column2	Column3	....
RowKey1	Value1	Value2	Value3		Value4	Value5	Value6	
RowKey2	Value A	...						

NoSQL Column Oriented Database Table Structure

As shown above, column oriented databases have the data organized in the following way. Each table will have a set of column families (Eg: ColumnFamily1, ColumnFamily2, etc,...) to have a partition between the data. Each column family can have multiple columns Column1, Column2 and so on ... Columns are dynamic i.e. each row can have a variable number of columns. In simple form you can think of the structure as

Map<RowKey, Map<ColumnFamily, Map<ColumnKey, Value>>>

To understand better let's take an example. Whenever we login to email applications like gmail, yahoo mail etc, we see a list of emails along with some meta information of the emails right. Since the growth of emails is very high, it's a good idea to store this data in NoSQL table structure. For this scenario the table structure can look like below.

- Table: EmailMetaData
    - rowKey : userId
    - columnKey : messageId
    - columnValue: email MetaData Object.
- Sample data can be :
    - Userid1 : (1234 :: metadata1), (2345 :: metadata2) ....
    - Userid2 : (8234 :: metadata4), (3445 :: metadata5) ....

As you can see, userid1 is the row key. Columnkey is 1234. Column value is metadata1. The columns can grow as much as possible.

So if you observe the above NoSQL table structure, the data can grow in two forms.

1. **Wide Column:** In this form data is stored dynamically in multiple columns. So the table width grows as the data grows.
2. **Tall Tree:** In this form as the data grows, the number of rows in the table keeps growing. This can be in addition to the dynamic number of columns. Since the table grows in a tall structure it's called tall tree form. In the above example the number of users also can grow along with individual user emails.

In case of column oriented databases, underlying frameworks are mostly designed to keep the data of all the dynamic columns close to each other in the same node or a nearby node. This improves the performance to a large extent.

Document Databases

In the case of a document database, all the data is stored in the form of documents. These documents can be termed as objects. Format of these objects can be in the format of JSON or database specific serialization. The values of these documents can be in any type like strings, numbers, objects etc. depending on what the user wants to store. These documents are grouped together in the form of collections. These databases have a flexible, semistructured, and hierarchical nature of documents and document databases allows them to evolve with application needs. MongoDB, CouchDB, and Amazon DocumentDB are good examples of document databases.

Graph Databases

Social networks are good examples of graph databases. In graph databases, data is stored in the form of graphs representing nodes and edges. Nodes can hold information such as places, people etc. Edges store the relationships between the nodes. If you ever wonder how you get friend suggestions on facebook or follow suggestions on twitter of some friend who is an indirect connection to you, this can be achieved efficiently with graph databases. In addition to social networks, Fraud detection, Recommendation engines are good use cases of graph databases. Neo4j, JanusGraph are good examples of graph databases.

How to choose a specific SQL or NoSQL database?

There are several factors involved in picking the right database for your application needs.

- CAP Theorem lays a good foundation for this. We will discuss the CAP theorem in the following section. Based on the CAP theorem we can eliminate various choices of different databases and weigh handful ones. Since we saw various guarantees of different databases, as mentioned earlier, CAP theorem can lay a good foundation for choosing a specific database.

- When it comes to picking between SQL vs NoSQL, another important driving factor is whether we need to have relationships between the data. If you want to maintain strict relations between the data SQL is a good option. If not you can go with NoSQL systems.
- One other important factor for choosing a database is scalability. NoSQL systems are designed to have more horizontal scalability compared to SQL systems. So if you need to have a system that can support heavy loads then it's a good choice to pick NoSQL for data storage.
- One benchmark observation between NoSQL vs SQL is that if the Queries per second is in the range of a few thousands per second, then SQL can be enough for the system. But if the QPS goes beyond 10K per second then it's a good idea to go with NoSQL systems. This is not a hard rule but a general observation across various systems.

Now that we know CAP theorem is one of the key factors for picking our databases, let's understand what it's all about.

CAP Theorem

CAP Theorem also called Brewer's theorem states that it is impossible for a distributed data store to simultaneously provide more than two out the three guarantees of *Consistency, Availability, Partition Tolerance (CAP)*. To understand more let's look at each of the properties.

Consistency

Distributed systems involve multiple nodes for serving the data. Let's say we are trying to write the data to our data store with multiple machines. When we try to write the data to each of the machines, if there is a read request that tries to access the latest written data from a node that doesn't have latest data, then the client will receive outdated data. Consistency is the property that ensures every read receives the most recent write or an error. Since replication is very important for fault tolerance, consistency plays a key role while the data is being replicated. Consistency can be of two types.

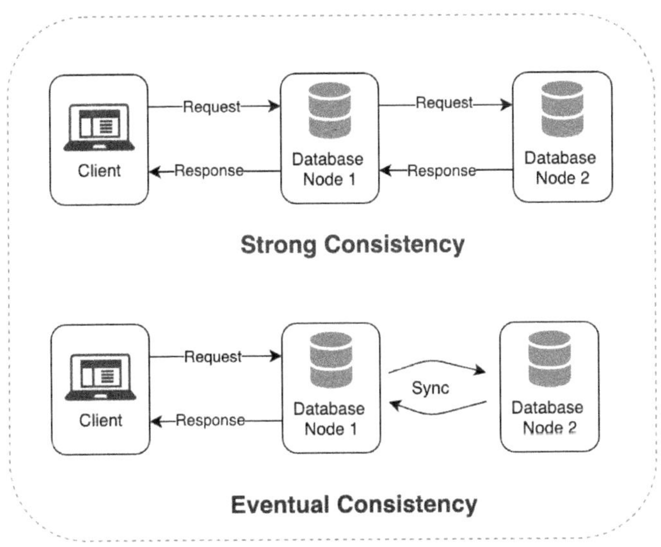

Strong Consistency Vs Eventual Consistency

1. Strong Consistency

Strong consistency guarantees the data is consistent across all the nodes for every write request. As shown in the image above, when a client makes a write request to Database Node 1, as part of the same request, the data is written to the database node2. Only after the data is written successfully to all the nodes, the response is given to the client with a success code or error code depending on whether the write is success or failure respectively. RDBMS is a good example of strong consistency.

2. Eventual Consistency

Eventual consistency guarantees that if an update is made to the data of a node then the updated value will be propagated ultimately to all the replicas of that node. From the image above, when a client makes a write request to the database node 1, once the data is saved in node 1 client gets a success response immediately. In the background, database node2 continuously syncs with datanode 1 in the background and eventually it gets the latest changes propagated. Since the consistency is happening in the background and changes may not be immediately available in all the nodes this can be termed as eventual consistency.

Availability

Availability indicates that every request receives a response from the system in a reasonable amount of time. In simple terms the system should be up and running all the time. Same applies at storage level too. Even though the data may not be the latest, the system should still be able to serve the requests without any downtime.

Partition Tolerance

System should continue to work despite the network failures between the components. There could be slight message loss or partial failures but most of the requests should succeed. One way to achieve partition tolerance is to do data replication across different networks and nodes to accommodate any outages. No distributed system is safe from network failures. Underlying storage systems should keep this point in mind while the design is being done.

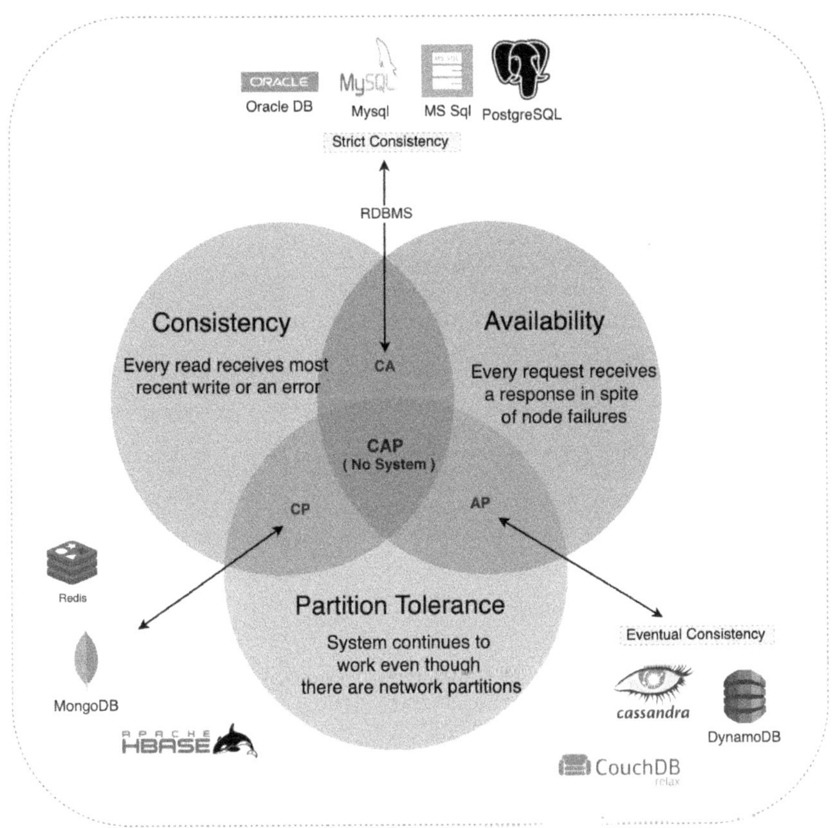

So CAP theorem says that it's impossible to build a system with all these three guarantees (Consistency, Availability, Partition Tolerance) simultaneously. As shown in the image above, only 2 of the 3 properties can be achieved in any system. The combinations can be CA, CP, AP which are marked in the image above. RDBMS is a good example of a system with CA guarantees. Examples of these systems are as follows.

CA: RDBMS Systems like MySQL, PostgreSQL, OracleDB, MS Sql etc.

CP: NoSQL databases like Redis, Hbase, MongoDB

AP: Eventually consistent databases like Cassandra, Amazon DynamoDB, CouchDB.

The intersection point of CAP doesn't have any systems as indicated.

8. Architecture Patterns

As the applications scale, the number of components and the number of servers that do the application processing grow substantially. Architecture patterns define a methodology in which the application servers can be organized and scaled. There are multiple ways to achieve it. Let's look at some of the popular ones.

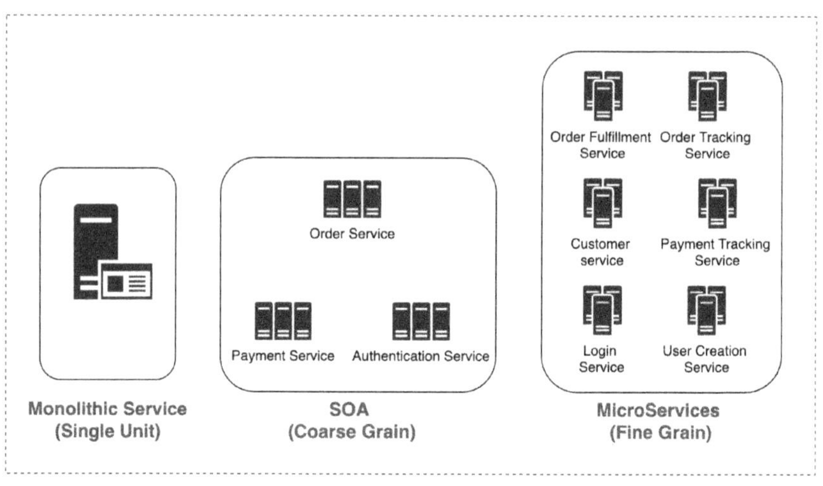

Architecture Patterns

1. Monolithic Architecture

Monolithic service has all the application modules tied together as one single service. Within the same service different modules execute sharing common resources across different modules. If we have to scale a monolithic system the whole service needs to be replicated to multiplier server instances. Code maintenance becomes very tough as the application grows and each module may require different scaling capacities which is not possible with monolithic architectures.

2. Service Oriented Architecture (SOA)

In a service oriented architecture, each module is divided into individual services. Each service can scale at its own by adding more instances specific to that module. In the above image, an ecommerce application can have multiple modules like Order Service, Payment Service, Authentication service etc. Modules are divided as per the functional domain. This division is not too granular and hence its kind of coarse grain architecture.

3. Microservices

If we divide service oriented architecture modules into much smaller modules we can scale each piece with great flexibility. Each service is divided into much more finer services serving specific needs. For example, Order Service itself can be split into multiple sub services like Order Fulfillment service, Order tracking service etc. Microservices are a great way to scale the applications. But since multiple services are involved, application complexity can grow a lot, which is the tradeoff we need to have for microservices.

Microservices and SOAs have multiple services interacting with each other. So communication between these modules is very important. To have a reliable communication some of the possible ways include

1. **Distributed Queues:** Each service publishes a message to a queue and listens to messages of incoming queues.
2. **HTTP Requests:** Each service can initiate a Http connection with another service thereby REST Apis can be exposed for interaction.
3. **Websockets:** Since HTTP requests involve TCP connection overhead, we can use Websockets too to maintain a persistent connection between the servers.

4. Serverless Architecture

Serverless architecture has become famous with the advent of the cloud era. It's a way to run and build the apps without the need for infrastructure management. Code execution is managed by the server without the developer worrying about server maintenance and provision. Code is written in stateless form in the form of functions and backend architecture manages the execution of these functions. AWS Lambda is one such example of serverless architecture. It is an event-driven, serverless computing platform provided by Amazon as a part of Amazon Web Services

9. Consistent Hashing

Before getting into consistent hashing let's learn some of the basics of Hashing. One of the most frequently used data structures is HashTable because of the average lookup time of O(1). In order to build a hash table we need a Key, Value and a function to generate the hash called Hash Function. Each key is passed onto a hash function which generates a unique value that can be put into one of the buckets. So when a look up happens the hash of the key is generated and value is queried from the hash buckets. When we think about a single machine system this works perfectly fine. But as our data grows, we need to have multiple machines to store the data. That's when Distributed Hash Tables come into picture. In a distributed hash table the data is hashed and stored in the form of key value pairs in multiple buckets. In addition to this the buckets can be split and spread across multiple servers in a network.

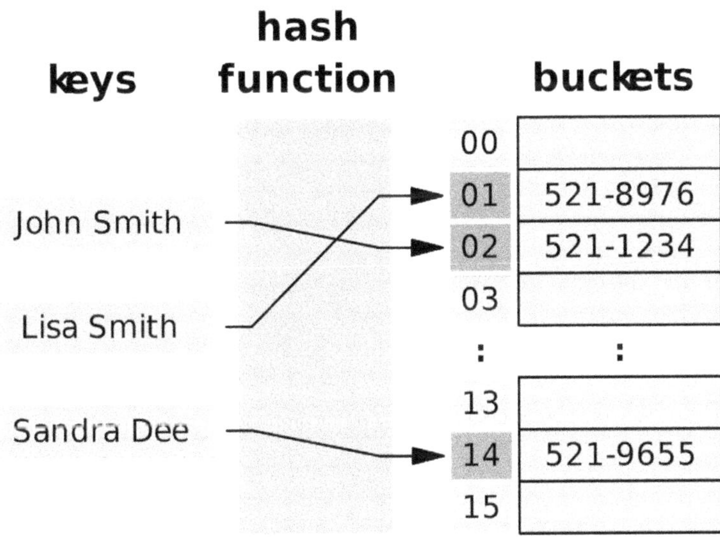

(Source Wikipedia: Hash Function)

So if we have N servers to hold our keys, then before querying the underlying bucket, we should first know which server a specific hash key belongs to before going at bucket level. In order to achieve this if the data is distributed uniformly across multiple servers, we can have a modular function like key % N in order to decide which server a specific key belongs to. As long as the number of servers N doesn't change, this approach works totally fine. But if we need to add a new server or if some server needs to be removed because it's crashed, we need to regenerate the hash values for all the keys and redistribute the hashes across a new set of servers. This approach is not efficient at scale. Consistent hashing helps solve this problem.

Consistent hashing is a special kind of hashing such that when a hash table is resized, only X/N keys need to be remapped on average where X is the number of keys and N is the number of slots/servers. To achieve this, let's say we have X number of keys and hash function H(X). When we hash all the keys lets say we get a range of values. Imagine we mapped these ranges of output values onto an edge of a circle. The values are spread across 0 to 360 degrees angle locations. Since we have N servers, if we apply the same hash function H(X) to the servers the range of these hash values will be similar to the range of hash keys. Mapping them on a circle results in the following setup.

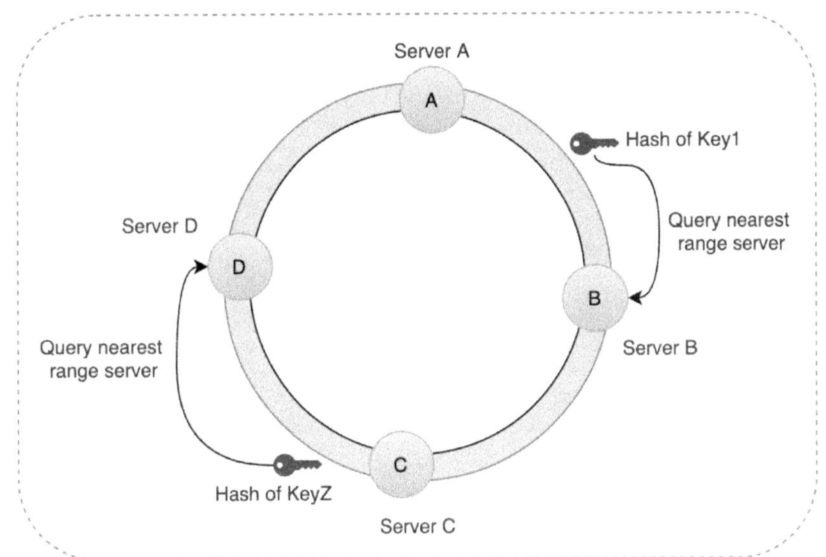

Consistent Hashing

If we map the Keys and Servers on the same hash function H(X) we can see them on the above circle ring. For a given Key, say Key1, the hash value comes in between the Node range A and Node range B as shown in the image above. So the server for Key1 would be the next highest hash range server B as shown. Similarly for KeyZ the next highest hash value server is Server D.

If we add a new server, say E between node D and node A, we need to just redistribute the keys within the servers D and A onto server E to balance the distribution. Similarly if we remove a node say A, we need to serve the keys from the neighbor nodes E and B. This way adding and removing nodes is easy in a consistent hashing system.

Jump consistent hashing is one other approach for consistent hashing efficiently. Many distributed NoSQL database systems and load balancers rely on consistent hashing for load distribution. Consistent hashing itself can be a vast topic to understand. You can refer to various reference as below:

Consistent hashing References:

https://www.toptal.com/big-data/consistent-hashing

https://arxiv.org/pdf/1406.2294.pdf

https://www.akamai.com/es/es/multimedia/documents/technical-publication/consistent-hashing-and-random-trees-distributed-caching-protocols-for-relieving-hot-spots-on-the-world-wide-web-technical-publication.pdf

Chapter 4

Must Learn Important Interview Question 1

URL Shortener service like TinyUrl/bit.ly/goo.gl

Now that we know the basic concepts of system design, let's look at some of the must learn interview questions to help with your system design interviews. First one to learn is URL shortener service.

1. Introduction & Requirement Analysis

URL Shortener service helps users share short urls across the web instead of long length urls. In a url shortener system, users input a long url and they should get an output of a shortened tiny url. When a user tries to access the tiny url it should redirect him to the original long url.

Eg: System Input - Long url: https://tipseason.com/how-to-read-file-as-string-in-java/

System Output - Tiny Url : https://tinyurl.com/35euu2cz

Functional Requirements:

1. User can enter long url and he should receive shortened url
2. User who tries to access shortened url should be redirected to the original long url page
3. User should be able to create custom tiny url for a long url
4. Short Url can contain characters of A-Z, a-z, 0-9 in the tiny url.

Non-Functional Requirements:

1. System should be highly available. If the system is down it means all the url redirections will fail. We should avoid that.
2. System is read-heavy and all read requests for url redirection should be with minimal latency. Read to write ratio can be 100:1.
3. System should support short url generations at scale with at least 10M write calls per day, i.e., 300M per month.

Optional Additional Requirements:

1. System can have analytics for url reads and writes.
2. Each url can have an expiry time.
3. System should have developer api support.

2. Capacity estimations

As per the current requirements, our system should support about 10M short url creations per day. Please refer to the cheat sheet for capacity estimation and easy calculations at (https://pramod.me)

Note: All calculations are approximate and averaged. ~ indicates approximation.

1. **Requests Per second:**
   - Writes: 10M/day = ~115 Requests/sec = ~100 Requests/sec
   - Reads: Read to write ratio: 100:1. So reads per day = 100* 10M/day = ~10K Reqs/Sec

   As an average, we can consider that our system needs to handle about 10K Reqs/sec

2. **Storage estimation:**
   - Assume long url average size : 2KB (2048 chars). Tiny Url : 7B(7 chars: We can only store the hash value eg: bit.ly/abcdef in db we can just store "abcdef", since the first part is fixed). Time stamp : 10B. In addition if we have other data, Approximate average size for data storage lets say: 2KB.
   - Url Storage: New urls per month = 10M * 30 = 300M. So size per month= 300M * 2KB = 600M KB = 6 * 10^8 KB = 6 * 100 GB = 600GB per month = 7.2TB per year = 36TB per 5 years.

What should be the length of TinyUrl?

From our requirements we are clear that the allowed characters in a tiny url are A-Z (26 count), a-z(26 count), 0-9(10 count) i.e. total 62 chars. So from 62 chars if we choose a length of about 7 characters we can generate about 62 ^ 7 = 3.5 Trillion urls which can take quite a bit of time to get exhausted. So we can choose **7 as our tinyurl length.**

3. API & Model Design

Now that we know what is the scale of the system that we are building, if we can define high level system APIs, it will help us clearly define the functional requirements in a more systematic way. For tinyurl, typical APIs include.

- String signupUser(User user)
- String createShortUrl(String userId, String actualUrl, String customUrl)
- String getActualUrl(String shortUrl)
- String deleteShortUrl(String shortUrl)

For simplicity, we are not focusing on Login and authentication for now

Data model can be as below:

- User: user Id*, user Name, creation Time, (Optional: password Hash, salt etc).
- Urls: short Url*, actual Url^, creation Time, userId^, (Optional: expiration Time).

* indicates Primary Key. ^ indicates Index key.

Note that the above model is not specific to any database. It represents the overall structure of data.

What storage to choose ? Is it SQL or NoSQL?

At this point, we have enough data to decide the type of database that we need to have. Some data points are

- 10K Reads / sec and 100Writes / sec. So overall queries per second are about 10K/sec.

- There need not be relationships between the data for the main logic of create and getUrls.
- We have about 300M writes per month.

Looking at above data points, we can say that the system should have about an average of 10K Queries per second support. Also the data doesn't require much joins for core APIs(get, create urls. We can ignore userId for all reads). Also since the system is more read heavy with about 10K Reads / sec, in order to use SQL based systems we might have to bring in the logic of Sharding and stuff which might add extra overhead. Keeping these things in mind it's better to have a NoSQL based system like Hbase / DynamoDB etc instead of SQL based systems. One other advantage of NoSQL systems is they natively have some kind of cache(eg: BlockCache in Hbase) for reads which can speed up our overall system.

* ***Tip:*** *If your system is supposed to handle queries at the rate of 10K per second then it's better to choose NoSQL. If the design is at a rate of about 10 to 100 queries per second, SQL could be a better choice as it has more advantages in terms of Select queries, Joins.*

4. Design & Scalability

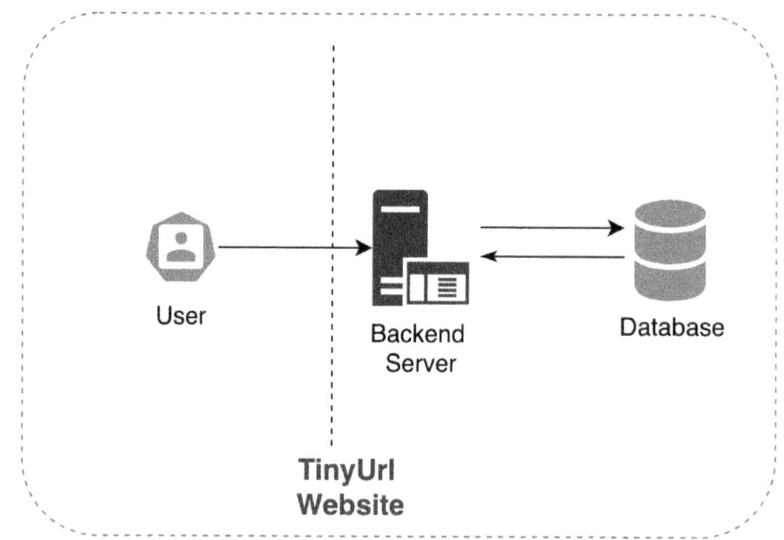

Naive System Design for TinyUrl

Let's get into the high level design for our tinyurl application.

- Let's have our users try to connect to our tinyurl application. In our case, users try to access the website through a browser or through a mobile site.
- As shown in the image above a naive solution to our tinyurl solution can be as follows: we need to have a backend server which can take user requests. Each request needs to go to our database from which the long url can be fetched or short url can be written.
- But is this production ready to scale for multiple users ? No.

So let's get into a more scalable design.

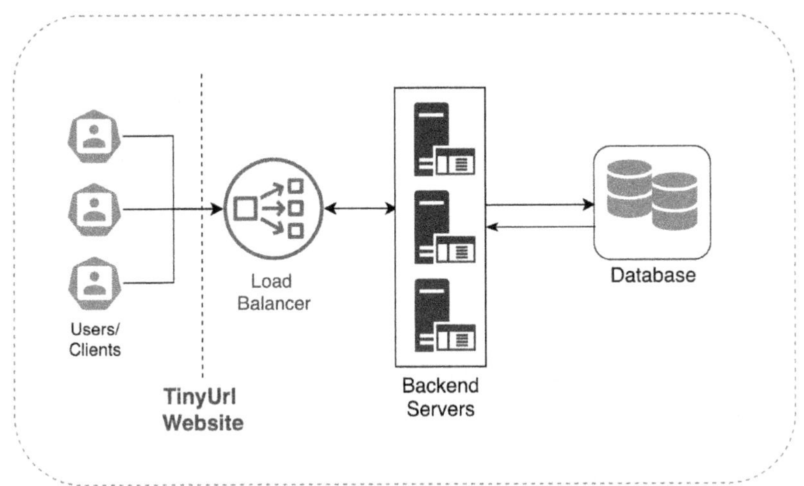

Basic System Design for TinyUrl

As the number of users grow, we need to have a more scalable system. The approach can be as follows.

- Since the number of requests per second is about 10K/sec, we should have multiple backend servers which can handle user requests concurrently.
- To provision multiple servers we should distribute the load to each of the servers. To do that, we need to have a load balancer which can direct the user requests to individual backend servers. Note that load balancer itself can be a cluster of servers whose job is to redirect the user requests to specific app servers.
- For simplicity, our load balancer can follow the strategy of a round-robin mechanism and distribute the load uniformly. (To know more about load balancer strategies refer to the load balancer section).

- Since our website needs to support browser requests and also in future we may have to support developer API support, we need to have some kind of standard mechanism for exchanging data. We can choose JSON format for structuring our data since it is more lightweight and developer friendly.

Typically all user requests should land on to backend servers via JSON payload using the HTTP protocol.

Once the backend servers receive the requests, they can either save or read the data from our database. As per our discussion in the previous section, we can choose a NoSQL database like Hbase/Cassandra/DynamoDB etc.

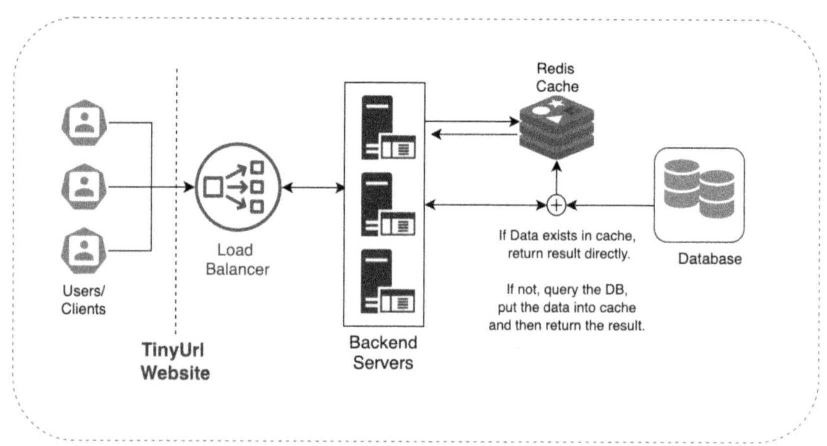

Read Path Optimization with Redis + NoSQL native cache

Read Path (How to get long url from short url)

During the */getActualUrl* call, we need to provide the original url from a short url. So our backend servers should query our database and get the original url from a short url.

Once we get the long url from the short url we can give the input back to the user/client with redirection headers which can then redirect the requests to the respective original url page.

- Since we are talking about a range of 10K Requests/sec and that our application needs to have very low latency we need to have some component which can provide faster reads and try to avoid DB disk hits.
- These faster reads can be achieved using a distributed caching system. So we can have a Redis / MemCache cluster in between the app servers and DB.
- For a specific user read request, if a long url exists in our cache, the server can directly return the result without hitting the DB. If the url doesn't exist in cache then the app server can fetch the data from DB, Put the data in our cache and then return the data to a user. This helps all subsequent read requests for the same url to be faster until the data exists in our Cache.
- We can choose the LRU/LFU mechanism for cache eviction policy.
- In addition to above cache, since our primary DB is NoSQL system, to provide faster reads, as discussed in Storage section, most NoSQL systems have some kind of internal caching mechanism like a Block cache (in case of Hbase) or Cassandra's built-in key and row caches which can provide faster data retrieval. These caches are at a DB level which will further improve the read performance.

Write Path: (How to convert long url to short url)?

For a TinyURL system design interview question, the write path is one of the main areas the interviewer wants to deep dive. So let's look at different approaches on how to convert a long url to short url at scale. Before getting into unique url generation, let's see

How to convert a long url to short url?

As per our capacity estimations, we have a url length of about 7 characters long. The possible characters are a-z (lets name them 0 to 25), A-Z (26 - 51), 0-9 (52 - 61). So 62 ^ 7 = ~3.5 Trillion combinations = ~43 bits.

43 bits can be converted into base 62 format (since 62 chars total) just like we convert decimal to binary which results in numbers between 0 to 61. Each of this number can be mapped to one of the characters in the above 62 allowed char list.

So if we can somehow generate a ***unique 43 bit number (let's call it id)****, this can be used as a short string for our tinyurl application! The core problem of designing a tinyurl system lies in the part of "How can we effectively generate this unique small id for a large string". So let's see how we can generate this id in our system.*

Approach 1: Random number generator

The straight away approach that comes to our mind is to generate a random 43 bit number and convert the result to string appending the domain and return back to the user. If the random number already exists in our database we can generate a new random number and this loop can continue until we find a unique number.

Problems with this approach:

1. The obvious problem with this approach is that it's simply not scalable. We might end up with a long loop that can run for a long time resulting in poor system performance.
2. This approach can also result in race conditions between app servers because it's possible that two threads or app servers can result in the same data being added to db because of get and put checks. To avoid this there should be DB level support to have a PutIfAbsent kind of mechanism which is not feasible in a NoSQL system.

Approach 2: Hash Based approach like MD5/ SHA1

Instead of generating a random number, we can apply a hash function(either MD5/SHA1) to the input url. MD5 hash results in about 128 bit length. Converting into base 64 encoding results in a 21 character long string. We can pick the first 7 characters out of this string to generate the unique url.

Eg: MD5(https://twitter.com/pramodnanduri/with_replies)= 8fccd82355d4a15bdce79e64e34ffbdf

Tiny url can be stored as : 8fccd82. Shortened url will be : tinyurl.com/8fccd82

Problems with this approach:

1. Most hash functions have a small chance of getting the same hash value for two different strings(Technically called as Collision). So if two different long urls result in the same hash value then we get into the same problem of not having a unique url.

    - Since this chance is a bit lower than approach 1, we can go with the approach of checking the database if the url exists; if not insert into DB.

2. But then, this approach can still have the race condition problem as stated in problems of Approach 1.

Approach 3: Offline Key generation service

Since the first 2 approaches have the same problem of race conditions between servers/ threads, a better way to handle this is to have an offline key generation service.

- We can have an offline key generation service(let's call it Key-Gen service) which can precompute the combination of 7 char length keys and store it in our database.
- We call it offline because these servers can work independently irrespective of user requests.
- The key-gen service can maintain a counter to generate urls one by one and store them in a database.
- Whenever a createUrl request comes, the Key-Gen service can return one of the unused keys and return back to the request.
- The Long -> short url request can query key-gen service for a unique key and map to long url and save it in our main database.

A good advantage with this approach can be that the keys can be generated asynchronously and without any restriction on the range.

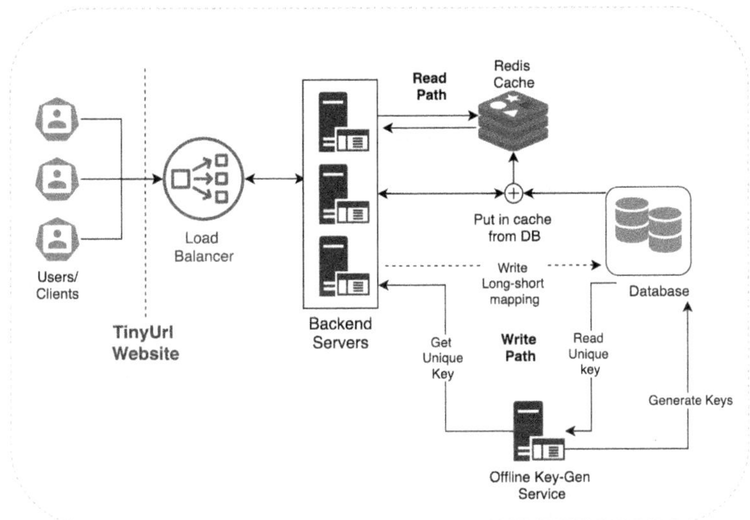

Write Path with Offline Key-Gen service

Problems with this approach

1. During high volume, there could be slight concurrency issues i.e. Key-Gen service can return the same url to two different requests.
   - Workaround for this would be that, whenever a uniqueUrl request is placed, key-gen service should mark the key as used and then only return the result back to the caller. In this way it guarantees a unique key is generated.
2. Key-Gen service can be a single point of failure. Since the number of write requests is about 100 /sec, if the key-gen service is down the whole write path is down.
   - A work around for this is to have a Standby key-gen service server which gets activated if the master server is down.

3. But then slowly as the system grows further, this key-gen server can become a bottleneck since it's mainly backed by a single server.

Approach 4: Counting Approach with custom token service

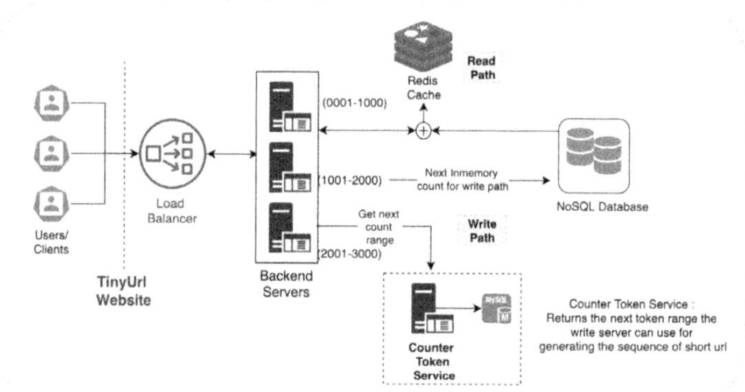

Counter Token service approach for converting to short urls

To avoid the problem of single point of failure of key-gen service, we should somehow distribute the load to multiple servers to generate unique tiny urls.

How does the counter approach work?

Counter approach works in the following way. Let's say we want to generate 3.5Trillion tiny urls. These urls can be generated sequentially using a counter one by one from 0 to 3.5 Tr right. As per our previous discussion if we can convert the next counter number into base64 we should be able to get the next unique tiny url. To do that at scale, we can't rely on one single server doing the count from 1 to 3.5Tr. Instead we should divide the counting numbers as ranges for eg: (1-1000), (1000-2000) etc.

So if we can distribute these ranges to multiple write servers they can generate these numbers sequentially using in-memory counters.

To distribute these ranges across multiple write servers we can have a counter token service.

- We can maintain a counter token service. The job of counter token service is to provide a range of unused numbers that can be used by write servers to generate sequences of tiny urls.
- Every write server should query the counter token service to get the next unused range of numbers during app server startup or when the current list is exhausted. These ranges can be used in-memory within the app servers
- Since the requests to Counter token service come only during write server startup or count exhaustion, the volume of requests that come to this service is low. So this service can be backed by a MySQL database to maintain unused count range with a few sets of servers and db instances.
- If we have to expand our counter to multiple geographical locations, we can split the range of counters and replicate the behavior of token service with individual ranges.

In this way, we can generate sequences of numbers by multiple servers during tiny url generation.

Since the numbers are unique there is no chance of having collisions for tiny urls.

Problems with this approach

1. Since each write server calculates the counts in memory, if the server goes down, we might lose track of where the

current counter is. So there is a chance of loss of range of counter numbers

- Since the number of urls are so high and we can always increase the counter range, losing a few numbers can be one tradeoff we can stick with.
- If needed, we can further minimize the loss by periodic reporting of used ranges to the counter token service.

Approach 5: Counting Approach with ZooKeeper(More advanced level)

Finally, if we want to simplify our counter token service logic, we can use a component called Zookeeper.

Zookeeper is a distributed coordination service which has abilities to detect if a specific server is down, watchers for data changes etc.

So instead of having our custom logic built from scratch for token service, we can have a Zookeeper based backend for our token service which can provide unused ranges based on zookeeper configuration. The behavior can be similar to the previous counter approach but the ability to detect a failed server or change in configuration can be propagated easily using zookeeper.

So now that we are clear on the read and write paths let's get into the next section.

5. Final Thoughts and Future Extensibility

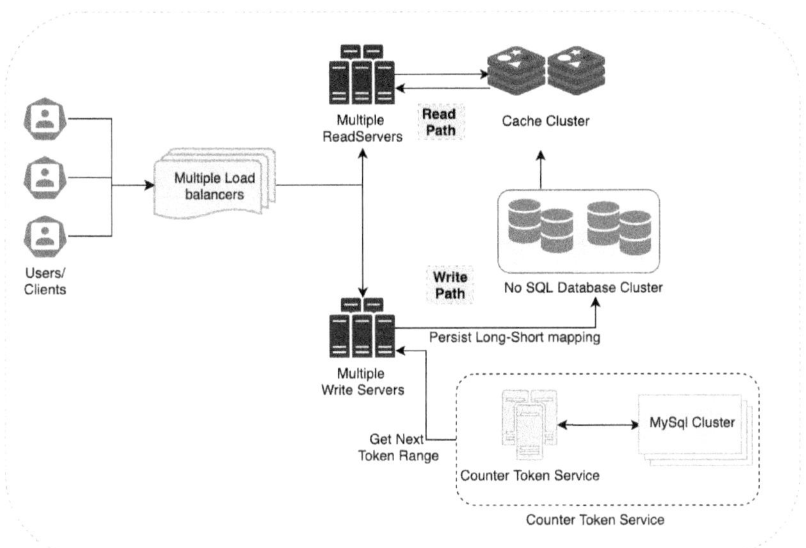

Complete Scalable Tiny Url System Design

So here is the fully scalable tiny url system design as shown in the image above.

- From our detailed design, we can see there could be multiple users with about 10K Requests per second. So it's important to have multiple load balancers and they can be added at different locations like app server level, cache layer level, token service level etc.
- The backend app servers can be further divided into write and read microservices so that read and write paths can be served independently.
- Cache needs to be a cluster of servers instead of a single redis instance.

- Custom token service should have multiple instances of token servers and mysql cluster
- We might have to introduce metrics like url hits, location etc, in future for read and write requests. So we can have an offline process for reporting and metric collection servers.
- Metric collection can happen during the request threads or they can also be achieved by querying url logs via elastic search.
- We should secure the system with appropriate privileges and each of the resources at DB level, app server level.
- If we have to expand our service to multiple geographical locations, we can have a CDN network for read and write requests.

Chapter 5

Must Learn Important Interview Question 2

Design News feed system like Twitter, Facebook

1. Introduction & Requirement Analysis

Modern social websites have a news feed system to display the timeline of activity that happens on the websites. Twitter has a news feed of tweets that serves as the home page. Facebook has a news feed of posts that gets displayed to every user based on his friends and like list etc.

Goal of this question is to design a news feed system like twitter, facebook etc.

For the purpose of the demonstration, we will discuss twitter system design with below requirements.

Functional Requirements

1. Users should be able to post a tweet.
2. Users should be able to see a timeline of relevant tweets.

3. Timelines can be divided into user timeline (list of tweets user made), home timeline (home page timeline for a user)
4. Users can follow other users

Non Functional Requirements

1. System should be highly available. If the system is down it means users won't be able to post a tweet or see the user timeline.
2. System is read-heavy and all read requests viewing tweets and user timeline should have very minimal latency. Read to write ratio can be 100:1.
3. Twitter currently has approximately 350M active users (as of 2021).
4. 6000 tweets/second are made on the platform every second. 600K Read Queries per second(QPS) for generating user timelines.
5. System can be eventually consistent i.e. it's ok if users can see the tweets from followers with a bit of delay.

Optional Additional Requirements

1. Users should be able to see the latest trends
2. Users can send private messages.
3. Users can search for tweets and search timeline can be displayed.
4. Tags timeline can be displayed.

2. Capacity estimations

As per the current requirements, our system should support about 6000 tweets per second. Please refer to the cheat sheet for capacity estimation easy calculations.

Note: All calculations are approximate and averaged. ~ indicates approximation.

1. **Requests Per second:**
   - Tweet Writes: 6000 Requests / sec. This is the number of new tweets. Each tweet might fan out to followers (we will discuss various strategies in the design section) = 500M Requests / day.
   - Tweet Reads: Let's assume Read to write ratio: 100:1. So tweet reads per second = 100* 6000 Tweets/sec = 600K Reqs/Sec
2. **Storage estimation:**
   - For twitter, the maximum size of each tweet = 140 characters =140 bytes.
   - So for 500M Req/day, we can have 500M/day * 140Bytes = 700 * 100 M Bytes / day = 70GB/day = 3.5TB/Month just for tweet content.
   - There could be other metadata storage like users, tags etc.

Since we are talking at the scale of about 600K read requests per second and about 6K write requests per second, it's better to have a NoSQL storage for the tweets.

3. API & Model Design

Since we know requirements and capacity estimates its time to jump into API & Model design for our twitter application. To formalize the requirements let's define the APIs driving the system. For simplicity we will skip signupUser and loginUser APIs.

- String createTweet(String userId, String tweetText)
- JSON getUserTimeline(String userId)
- JSON getHomeTimeline(String userId)
- Boolean followUser(String userId, String followUserId)

Data Model

From the capacity planning, we know that NoSQL storage is the right mechanism for storing the tweets information. So we can use NoSQL for tweets and some meta tables in MySQL. Here is how a data model can look like.

SQL Based Schema Design

- User: userId*, userName, creationTime, email, passwordHash (Optional salt etc).
- Tweet: tweetId*, userId^, tweetText
  - UserId should is a foreign key to userId and has one to many relationship
- Timeline: userId*, tweetId
- Followers: userId*, followerId^.
  - followerId is nothing but the userId of the person who is following.

If you are interested in how data can be stored specifically in NoSQL based design, you can use the below schema.

NoSQL Based Schema Design

For NoSQL based schema design we can design the table in various ways. Hybrid way of using both sql + nosql combinations is the best fit.

- User table, Followers table can be SQL tables as specified in SQL based schema above.
- Tweets, UserTimeline tables can be stored in NoSQL as below.
- Tweet table:
    - tweetId : rowKey
    - tweetId : some constant to represent a columnKey.
    - tweetObject: columnValue. tweetObject can have different metadata like userId, tweetText etc.
- Home Timeline table:
    - userId : rowKey
    - timeStamp: columnKey
    - tweetId : columnValue
- User Timeline table:
    - userId: rowKey
    - timeStamp: columnKey
    - tweetId : columnValue

To learn more about the NoSQl design please go through the NoSQL section of this book.

* indicates Primary Key. ^ indicates Index key.

User : userId(PK), name, email, creationDate, lastLogin

Tweet : tweetId(PK), data, location, creationDate

Follow : userId1, userId2

4. Design & Scalability

Since the main focus of the question is about how we can efficiently generate NewFeed, we will discuss various approaches starting with a basic approach and how we can improvise the same.

Approach 1: Basic Naive Approach

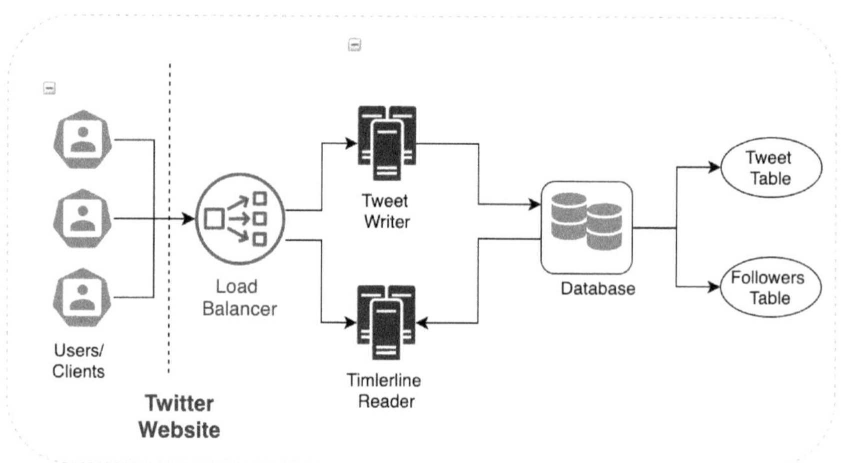

Approach 1 : Basic System Design for Twitter

- Let's have users connect to our twitter website. Since the number of users is high, one server is not enough. So we need to have a load balancer which can take incoming user requests and redirect the traffic to two sets of microservices.

One is the tweet writer service and second is the timeline reader service.

- Tweet writer service handles the processing of all new tweets, replies or retweets posted into the system. It's essentially the write path. When a new tweet is posted, tweet writer service takes the tweet and stores the data in the global tweets table.
- Timeline reader service handles the read requests. It basically handles the timeline generation for the user. When a user accesses his timeline, the request lands into the timeline reader service. For a given user it fetches the list of all the users current user follows. Gets the latest list of tweetIds of all the tweets that were posted by the following users. Queries the tweet database and gets the list of tweets data and populates the user timeline.

Problems with this approach

At a first cut, this system works. But we are talking about millions of users and each user can follow thousands of other users. So for a user who is following about 1K other users, timeline service should basically go through all the 1K following user tweets and fetch the tweet content and populate the timeline. All this needs to happen at read time. So it can be a case the user timelinc can load forever.

So let's get into a more scalable design.

Approach 2: Fanout Model

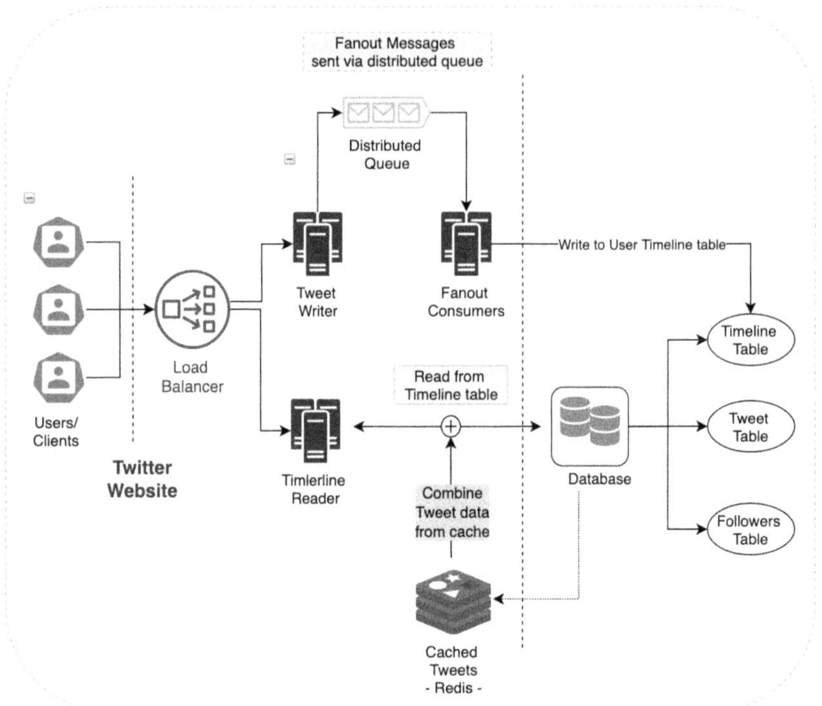

Twitter Timeline System design

Write Path

- In this approach instead of doing the timeline processing at user read time, we do it during the tweet write time.
- When a new tweet comes into the system, the tweet writer service saves the tweet into the tweet database. In addition to it, the tweet writer sends a fanout event i.e. a notification to the internal system saying a new tweet has arrived. Fanout event is basically a system message that gets published into a distributed queue so that consumers can process them asynchronously.

- A set of tweet consumers can listen to this distributed queue to process the fanout message. A tweet consumer reads the message to get the userId, tweetId. For the given userId, the consumers will fetch the list of all the followers for the user and put the tweetId into each of the user timeline tables. Note that tweet consumers can be part of the tweet writer servers or they can run as an independent server grid. Main goal is to make them have asynchronous processing threads.
- So basically we are precomputing the follower user timelines for every new tweet or retweet, so that the read performance can be faster. Since we can configure fanout consumers as many as we can, the delay for timeline population can be reduced. In addition we can have priority queue logic to prioritize consumption for important users.

Read Path

- When a user accesses the timeline, since the user timeline is already precomputed, timeline service basically gets the latest tweetIds of the current user and fetches the tweet content from the global tweet store and displays the list of tweets.
- Now that we know tweetId to tweetContent is stored in a database, hitting the disk everytime can affect the read performance. So for all the tweets, we can maintain a distributed cache like REDIS to store the tweetId to tweetContent and some other metadata in memory. This way read time can be drastically reduced.

Problems with this approach

For a normal user this approach works perfectly fine. But what if the user who tweeted has millions of followers i.e. a celebrity user ? In this case tweet writer service should basically write the tweet to all the millions of followers, which is not scalable and the destination users can have a significant delay in receiving celebrity tweets.

So let's see how we can optimize this.

Approach 3: Optimized approach

Approach 2 works totally fine for normal users. In the case of celebrity users we need to do some optimizations.

- Except for celebrity users, for regular users (users with follower count < n where n can be configurable at system level) like in approach 2 we will precompute the user timeline.
- When a user accesses his/her timeline, timeline service takes the list of precomputed tweets the user already has, in addition gets the list of celebrities the user follows and the latest tweets at read time like in Approach 1 but only for celebrities. In short
    - Usertimeline = Precomputed timeline + List of celebrity tweets the user follows.
- Also since the celebrity tweets are the most accessed ones, their tweets can be completely cached.
- So merging those tweets at user read time would be faster.

5. Final Thoughts and Future Extensibility

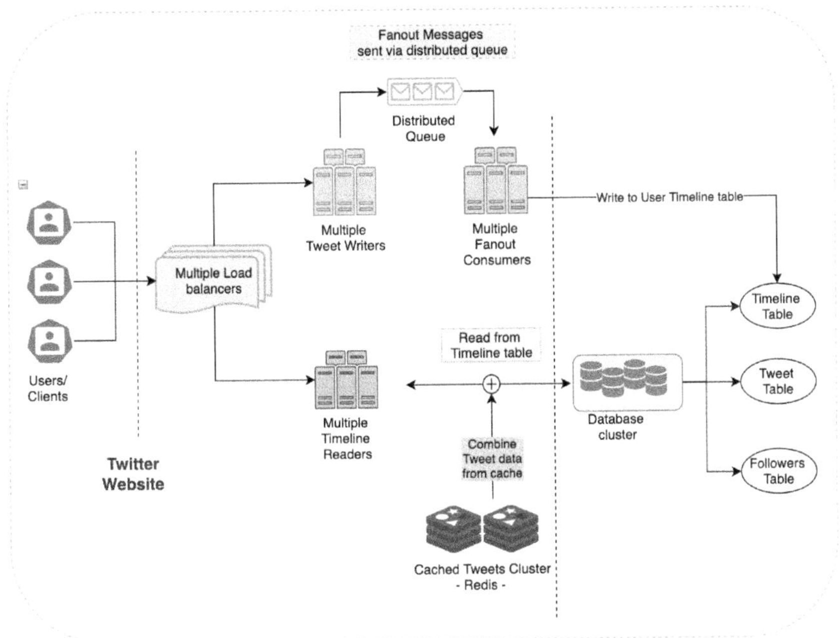

Fully Scalable Twitter Timeline System design

Now that we know how we can optimize the user timeline generation process let's get into how we can make it further scalable.

- From our capacity estimations, we can see there could be multiple users with about 600K Requests per second. Generating timelines at this scale needs to be further optimized inorder to be more scalable
- One way to optimize is to generate timelines only for users who logged into the website in the late 15 days or some configurable number of days. In that we don't generate timelines for inactive users.

- Cache needs to be a cluster of servers instead of a single redis instance since we are talking about high cache hits for tweet data.
- All the servers need to be multiple in number in order to have fault tolerance and horizontal scaling.
- Since we have very high traffic requirements, it's important to have the system requests served near to the user as much as possible. So we can have a CDN to serve the user content with the nearest geographical location possible.

Now that you know how to design the overall twitter user timelines, the same designs can be applied to any kind of news feed service. For example, for facebook news feeds we can post writers and timeline readers which can simulate the behavior of tweet writer and timeline reader respectively. When an interviewer asks you to design a timeline service of any sort try applying similar concepts and explain to the interviewer. Depending on the domain (website), you can change the respective entities (posts, tweets, instagram image feed etc.).

References

http://highscalability.com/blog/2013/7/8/the-architecture-twitter-uses-to-deal-with-150m-active-users.html

https://www.infoq.com/presentations/Twitter-Timeline-Scalability/

Chapter 6

Must Learn Important Interview Question 3

Design instant messaging service like Whatsapp or Facebook Messenger

1. Introduction & Requirement Analysis

Real time chat applications like whatsapp, facebook messenger, slack, telegram etc., have become part of our everyday lives. We often communicate with each other via these systems. In this chapter we are going to learn about how to design instant messaging systems like whatsapp, telegram etc. The reason these applications are called real time is because we see the messages flowing through the system almost instantly in spite of the messages traveling across various internet systems. Beyond the scenes there are interesting architectural components that are driving the whole system. Since whatsapp is one of the most frequently asked system design questions, lets focus on its system design. Note that this design can be extended to most chat based applications.

Functional Requirements

1. Users should be able to chat (send real time messages) with each other privately.

2. Users can send or receive group messages to multiple people. Almost 200 people can be part of the same group.
3. Users can send media like images, videos etc.
4. Messages status like sent, delivered, read receipts should be supported.
5. System should keep track of user online/offline status.

Non Functional Requirements

1. Message delivery should be real time or with very minimal delay.
2. System should be highly available. If the system is down it means users won't be able to send or receive messages which is a big problem.
3. System should be highly reliable i.e. the messages should not be lost at any instant.
4. Order of message delivery needs to be maintained i.e. the system is highly consistent.

Optional Additional Requirements

1. Messages need to be encrypted end to end in order to maintain privacy across the platform.
2. System should support disappearing messages after a certain timeout.

Whatsapp Vs Other Messengers

One interesting aspect to note about whatsapp is that, the messages in whatsapp are maintained in the server only until the message is delivered to the user. So lets say a user changes his app from one phone to another phone he can only restore messages from past backups that are either done on a drive or through iCloud for apple. We can't access all the past messages stored on the server. This is contrary to facebook, slack or telegram. In these apps, when a user upgrades his phone or app or moves to a different client we can retrieve the full chat history from the server.

2. Capacity estimations

More than 65 billion messages are sent daily via WhatsApp with about 2 Billion active users per month. (Rough figures obtained from the internet sources).

With the above numbers in mind, let's calculate some of the critical metrics that we need to design our system.

Note: All calculations are approximate and averaged. ~ indicates approximation.

Also Please refer to the cheat sheet for capacity estimation and easy calculations.

1. **Requests Per second:**
    - Number of messages flowing through the system = ~65 Billion / day = 2.7Billion / hour = ~0.75Million / second. So roughly we are dealing with about 1 Million messages per second that we need to take the messages from sending users and send to the target users.
    - Number of active users per month = 2Bn / month = 2 / (30 * 24 * 3600) per second = 0.77K per second = ~800 active users per second.

2. **Storage estimation:**
    - Assume the average text message size is about 200 characters. So it comes to about 0.2KB size (excluding the media content like images, videos etc). So for 1 million messages per second we have = 1Mn * 0.2 KB = 10 ^ 6 * 0.2KB = 0.2 * 10 ^ 3 MB = 200 MB per second.
    - So in a day it's about 200MB * 3600 per hour = 720GB per hour = 17280GB per day = 17.2TB per day = 6278 TB per year = 6.2PB per year = 31PB per 5 years.

From the high level estimates, we can see that we are dealing with about 1 Million messages per second and about 200MB per second storage. This shows that the system should be extremely scalable to support a wide traffic range. So let's look at how we can model our APIs and storage for the same.

3. API & Model Design

Before jumping into the core design, let's look at a systematic way of defining the functional requirements. As mentioned before this step helps have a clear definition of what requirements we are dealing with.

For message sending side:

- String sendMessage(String fromUser, String toUser, String content, String mediaUrl) : returns messageId
- String sendMessageToGroup(String fromUser, String toGroupId, String content, String mediaUrl) : returns messageId
- boolean isUserOnline(userId)

- String uploadMedia(String userId, Object media) : returns uploaded url
- Object downloadMedia(String mediaUrl) : returns media object.

On the client side once an event is received from the server as part of connection, we need to handle incoming requests. The event representations can be as follows.

- void on Message Received (String from User, String to Group Id, String msg Id, String content, Object Media)
- void on Message Status (String msg Id, Status status Type)
    - Status Type can be: DELIVERED, READ.

Data Storage

From the capacity planning it's clear that we are dealing with about 1 Million messages per second. So choosing a NoSQL storage is the best solution for the storage. Let's see how we can model the tables.

- User: userId*, userName, creationTime, email, phoneNumber, passwordHash (Optional salt etc).
- Groups: groupId*, groupName, groupDescription, groupImageUrl
- UseGroup: groupId*, userId
- Messages: This is in NoSQL Tables.
    - rowKey: msgId
    - columnKey : Constant
    - columnValue : MessageObject
- Message objects can have multiple attributes like : msgContent, mediaHash etc.

4. Design & Scalability

In a general web application,mostly we deal with single user/ client management. When we search for something on google a request is sent to the server and the response comes back to the same client. But in case of chat applications user A can send a message to user B right. So basically we are dealing with interactions between multiple users and clients. How should we maintain connection between two users and send messages between them ? Think about it for a few mins and then dive into the details below.

Approach 1: The Naive approach

Since we need to send messages between clients, we can follow this naive approach.

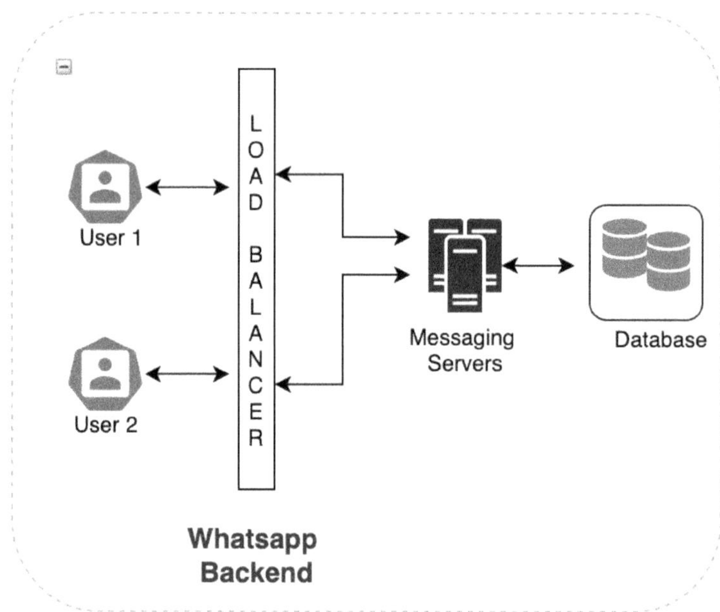

Approach 1 : Naive System design for whatsapp

Let's say we have two users: user1, user2 connected to whatsapp system via a load balancer.

- When user1 sends a message to user2, the message goes through the load balancer and reaches the messaging server via regular Http request.
- Messaging server takes the message and saves the message in database tables.
- In order for user2 to receive the message, the client can periodically connect to the messaging server to see if there is any message. Server checks that there are new messages in the database based on the last sync time and sends the messages to user2.
- If we configure periodic fetch time to say 500 ms or 1 sec any new messages can be delivered with minimal delay.

Problems with this approach

Of Course there are tons of problems with this approach. Couple of them are

- System is not fully real time. There is a lag between the messages for delivery.
- System is not fully scalable with this approach. Because if there are billions of users connecting to the system every 1 second system and backend database won't be able to scale at this level.

So let's see a better approach than this.

Approach 2: Scalable design

Since we need to send messages across different clients (user1 to user2) in real time, it's important to keep them connected to each other unless there is some network interruption if a user goes offline. One way to do it is to establish a peer to peer connection with each other i.e. if a user1 to user2 message needs to be sent then we can establish a connection to user2 and keep it open using a direct connection. After a bit of workaround on device discovery and stuff, it's feasible to do this but think about a scenario where you want to support group messages. How do you connect many people to each other ? How to manage if one client goes offline etc.

So instead of having clients connected to each other, we can make them connect via backend connection handling servers. Let's look at how we can do connection handling

Connection Handling

Client to Server Live Connections

So our goal is to connect user1 to user2 via a backend server. We will refer to user1 with u1 and user2 with u2 for easy convention.

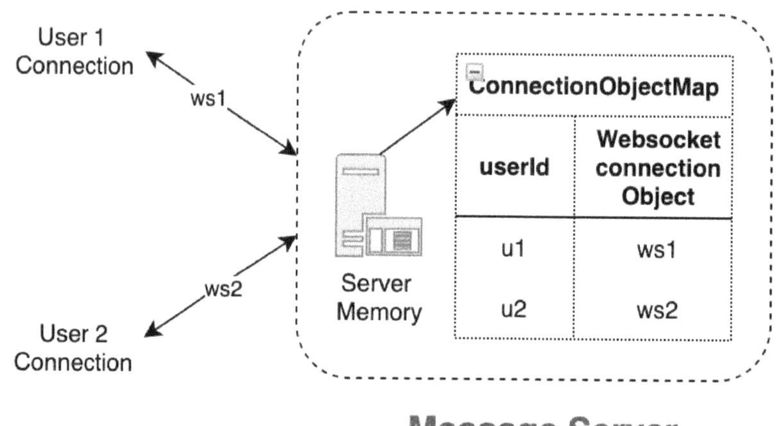

So if user1 needs to send a message to user2, in that case user1 establishes a connection to our message server. Same applies to user2 for message reception and then reply to the chat message. So essentially both user1 and user2 are connected to our backend Message Servers. Message servers do connection management across clients and deliver messages across each other. They keep the connection alive with the clients so that there can be real time message delivery across clients.

Regular HTTP requests go via TCP connection i.e. a client needs to initiate a TCP connection with the server and send the request for which server responds with a response. But in our chat applications, when a server receives a message from user1 it needs to send the message to user2 via the same connection. How is it possible ? Websockets are the best fit for this usage. (Refer to websockets chapter for more details).

- Websockets help us maintain a bidirectional connection between a server and client and that connection can be kept open until one of them closes the connection or if there is some network partition.
- When a user1 connects to the Message server via websocket a backend thread gets spawned on the server to handle the user connection. To keep track of the connected user to a server, in an in-memory Map (say ConnectionObjectMap) with key as userId and value as websocket connection object. So u1, ws1 map entry is created in server memory upon connection. Same can happen for user2. When a connection is disconnected this map entry can be removed.
- Our message payload JSON can look like below
    - { “from”:”u1”, “to”:”u2”, “message”:”message content” }

- Since the message contains the information about which user to send in, the message server can look up the ConnectionObjectMap with key = u2 which results in a connection object for the destination user if he is connected already. So the server can send the message to the user2 in the same connection. If the user2 is offline at the time of message, we will discuss this in the next section.

This works perfectly fine if there is only one messaging server. What happens if there are multiple servers with multiple users at scale ? How do we manage connections? Let's dive into this.

Multi Server Setup

As per our capacity estimations, since our scale is very large with about 800 users per second we need to have multiple servers handling the user connections simultaneously. Each of these connections needs to be open for a long time for real time communication.

Let's say we have n servers. user1 is connected to server1 and user2 is connected to server2. When a message is sent from user1, how do we know which server the message needs to be sent to out of given n servers ? In order to handle this, we need to maintain a common storage to look up the specific server for which the target user is connected to. Since we need to have this lookup as fast as possible and that this data is frequently changing per connection, we can maintain this storage in a redis cluster.

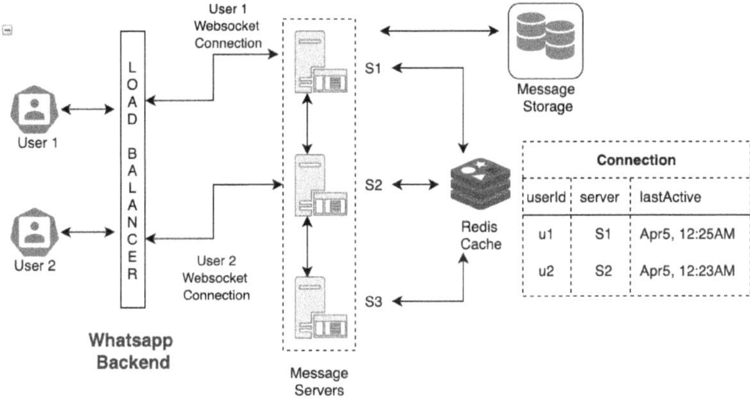

Whatsapp System design - Connection Handling

So whenever a user connects to a server, in addition to the in-memory ConnectionObjectMap, we can have a redis storage that keeps track of userId, serverId. The data structure can look like below.

Connection		
userId	server	lastActive
u1	S1	Apr5, 12:25AM
u2	S2	Apr5, 12:23AM

We can have a userId as key and value can be an object with serverId and lastActive time. We will discuss "lastActive" time in the "Last seen" section.

So when a user1 sends a message, the message server queries redis to find which server user2 is connected to using the above Connection table and returns the serverId to the message server S1. Once the server is known the message is sent to the target server S2 with the message payload we discussed before. Once server S2 receives the message, since it knows which user it needs to send via ConnectionObjectMap, it sends the message to the target user using the websocket connection.

Server to server connection

In the above step, we saw that server S1 needed to send a message to server S2. How can this happen? We can do this in two ways.

1. **Server-Server websocket connection:** Yes we can achieve this. Just the way we maintained a client server websocket connection, we can always connect each of the servers to other servers via a websocket connection. In that way the message can be sent in real time.
2. **Distributed Queue:** Since we are dealing with millions of messages it's tough to hold so many messages in app server memory while the transmission is being done. So we can have an intermediate distributed queue that each of the servers can send and listen to. So server S1 sends the message to a queue specific to server S2. Server S2 can continuously listen to the queue and deliver the messages. If there are hundreds of servers with billions of users, this is a very good option to scale the system.

Recipient User Online

While discussing the connection handling, we assumed that both the sender and receiver are online. So our connection handling can work seamlessly. If we choose the distributed queue option as the above step, we can guarantee the messages are not lost during the transmission.

Recipient User Offline

Now what if the receiver is offline ? We still need to guarantee messages are delivered right ? In order to do that, we need to introduce persistent storage for messages. So this can be worked out in this way.

- When user1 sends a message, we can first put an entry in our persistent storage. Then check if the user is online or not.
- If the user is online, a message can be delivered to the user and delete the entry from persistent storage. If the user is offline we will not remove the entry.
- When the user2 comes back online after a certain point of time, the message server can read through the persistent storage of what messages are not delivered and deliver them to the user. Once the delivery is complete, messages can be cleaned up.
- It's important to update the Redis Connection keys, ConnectionObjectMap entries in sync once the server adds or removes a client.

Persistent Storage apps

In the case of whatsapp as we discussed in the requirements section, since the messages are not persisted after delivery, the above system works totally fine. In the case of persistent apps like telegram, facebook messenger etc, the persistent storage that we discussed in the above section can be used to maintain the overall chat history. Instead of deleting the entry from storage when a message is delivered, we can keep it as it is. We can expose rest apis to retrieve this history of messages. Since the volume of messages is so high we can have a NoSQL storage system to persist all the messages for each of the users.

Last Seen

Whenever a user opens our chat app and reads his messages, we can mark the user as online. When a websocket connection is made to a messaging server, in order to keep the connection open for a long time with the server, the client can send a periodic tiny message like a ping message to the server saying it is online. We call this a heartbeat message. When a server receives the heartbeat message it can update the redis connection keys to mark the "lastActive" with the latest timestamp. This way we can detect if a user is online or not. Now let a userA be online. When userB opens the userA contact on whatsapp, the app can query the backend to get the latest status of userA from the redis cluster. This can indicate if the user is Online and the Last Seen time.

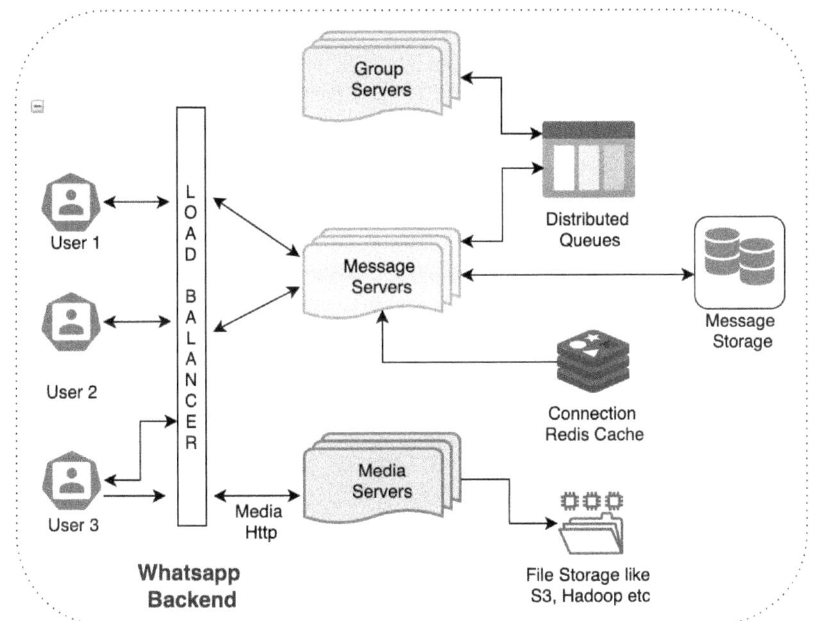

Whatsapp Design - Media + Group Handling

Media

Until now, we dealt with sending text messages across the users. But in real world chat applications, users will be able to send media files like images, videos, documents etc. How can we achieve this? To do this,

- When a user1 wants to send a media file to a recipient, the client asks for the media file location from the user filesystem.
- App can make a rest api Http call to our backend servers to upload media files onto the server. As discussed in the API section, the signature can look like this:
    - String uploadMedia(String userId, Object media) : returns uploaded url

- So we can have a set of backend servers, let's call them Media Servers, which can take user media and save the media on our backend file based storage like Amazon S3 or some Hadoop cluster.
- Once the backend server saves the media, it returns a url or a unique hash to the user as part of the upload request.
- Now when a user1 sends a message to the user2, as part of the message payload, we can send the url hash to the user2. The payload can look like this.
    - { "from":"u1", "to":"u2", "message":"optional message content", mediaUrl: "url or a unique hash for specific media" }
- On the receiving side user2, once the message is received, the client can read the message to check the mediaUrl. If the mediaUrl is present it can trigger a backend request to the media servers to download the media from the url or the unique hash.
- Note that, these media upload or download requests can be regular HTTP requests independent of the websocket connections that client maintains.

Group Chats

There is no fun if we don't have groups in our chat apps right! :-). In the real world most of the message transmissions happen through group messaging. That's why we see a lot of restrictions about how groups can be used to prevent system abuse. Let's look at how group chats can be handled.

We can modify the message payload a bit as below.

{ "from":"u1", "to":"groupId", "isGroup" : "true", "message":"optional message content", mediaUrl: "url or a unique hash for specific media" }

We can introduce a new variable isGroup which can indicate that the message is being sent to the group. Alternatively we can completely check if the message is a group or individual message based on the "to" field lookup in UserGroup tables on the backend.

- Once a user1 sends a message to group1, our message servers detect if the message is an individual message or a group message. Once the message server finds its group message, it routes the message to a separate set of servers called group servers.
- This routing can happen via server-to-server connection or through a distributed queue.
- Group servers are an extension to message servers. When a group message is received, lookup the group from the UserGroup table to get the list of users that are part of the group.
- For the group, it iterates each of the users and looks up the server, a target user is connected to and sends the message to the message server which can handle the target user via a websocket or a distributed queue.
- Message persistence can also happen for the received messages just like the individual message persistence handling.

The UserGroup table can have table structure as shown in the Model design section.

5. Final Thoughts and Future Extensibility

Since we have a lot of distributed components across the system there are few areas which we need to improve to achieve future extensibility.

Message Statuses

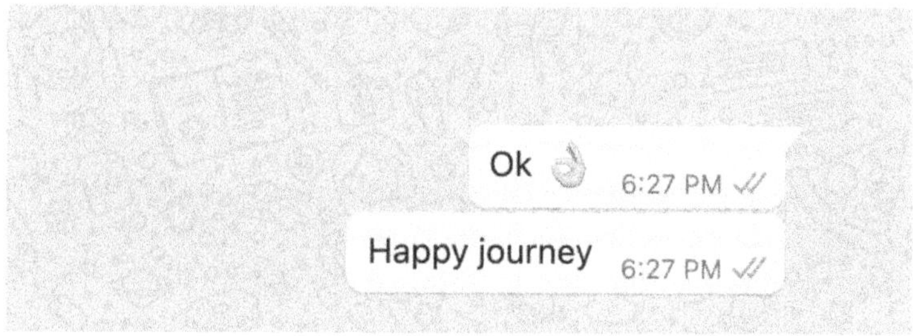

Modern chat applications track a message right from sending until the recipient reads it. Whatsapp shows three different statuses to a message.

1. Sent : Single Tick
2. Delivered : Double Tick in gray color.
3. Read : Double Tick in blue color.

To implement this in our system

- Once user1 sends a message to the server, when a server receives the message via websocket connection it can send an acknowledgement to the client saying the message is received. That's when the client can show a Single tick.
- Once the incoming server S1 processes the message and sends the message to the target server S2, target server S2 delivers the message to the user2 client and puts an entry

in the distributed queue with a deliveryStatus message. Delivery status message can have the following format :

{“messageId” : “abc123”, “status”:”SENT” }

- S1 can listen to this deliveryStatus queue and since the sending user is connected to this server, it can send a deliveryStatus event to the user1 via the websocket connection. Client of user1 can render the status on the UI.
- Similarly, let’s say user2 opens the message and reads the message, the client can send a websocket deliveryStatus event to the backend Server saying user2 has read the message. All these processes happen in the background without user intervention.
- Once the background event is received it can send that event to the user1 client.

Since each of the status sync events needs to happen irrespective of each user being online, we need to persist these states in our backend storage. So we can add respective tables in the database.

End to End Encryption

User privacy has become an important aspect for modern applications. Everyone across the internet feels like their data needs to be protected from being misused. So we might have to integrate end to end encryption to our service. What does that mean ?

When a message is sent from user1 to user2, this message needs to be encrypted right from the point of origin till the message is received by the client. The decryption should happen only at the target user client level. In order to achieve this we can have public and private key concepts similar to SSL encryption. For user1, the message is encrypted with the public key of user2.

The message is sent to the server. On the server there is no need to decrypt the message's actual content. On the recipient side i.e user2, since the message is encrypted with the public key of user2, it has a one to one mapping of private key with its public key. So decryption can be done using the private key. In this way we can guarantee the message is not decrypted anywhere in between the transmission.

Since we have base design in place, we can always extend various new application features as well as scalability features. Discussing above concepts thoroughly with your interviewer will keep you in a very good position with your interviewer. Just to remind you again, drive the whole discussion from your end and ask questions to your interviewer at each step. Good luck with your next interview :-)

References

https://developers.facebook.com/videos/f8-2016/a-look-at-whatsapp-engineering-for-success-at-scale/

Chapter 7

Must Learn Important Interview Question 4

Design video streaming service like Netflix, Youtube, Prime videos

1. Introduction & Requirement Analysis

Online video streaming has become one of the integral parts of our lives. Big apps like Netflix, Youtube etc, host tons of videos where users view them every second. If we have to do a system design for a video streaming service like Netflix or Youtube or amazon prime videos. How can we do that ? Let's go step by step.

Discussing every single aspect of a video service may not be possible in a 45 minutes interview. So make sure you discuss with your interviewer on specific requirements. For the scope of our discussion let's focus on following requirements.

Note that most concepts for Netflix and Youtube can be designed in the same manner. One difference to note is that netflix doesn't allow end users to upload videos. Only the site owners can upload videos on the backend.

We will try to cover the design for most common video platforms. For the purpose of the discussion, we will consider Youtube as our primary video platform.

Functional Requirements

1. Users will be able to watch a video.
2. Users can upload videos to their channel (for youtube)
3. Admins should be able to upload videos from backend (for Netflix)
4. Users will be able to search for videos
5. Users should be able to comment on videos.

Non Functional Requirements

1. Videos should be streamed without significant lag i.e. low latency.
2. System should be highly available: You don't want Netflix to be down when you are watching a movie.
3. System should be highly reliable: Videos that are uploaded should not be lost.

Optional Additional Requirements

1. Users should be able like or dislike videos
2. Each video should have a global rating of how good the movie is.
3. System should support analytics like number of views, current viewing count etc.

2. Capacity estimations

The scale of video platforms like youtube, netflix is very big. Youtube currently has 2.3 billion monthly active users.

Note: Please refer to the System Design cheat sheet for easy calculations.

~ indicated approximated to nearest zero (http://pramod.me)

Let's say we have 600 Million daily active users per day with each user watching about 10 videos per day.

1. **Requests Per second**
   - With 600Mn with 10 videos per day = 600M * 10 per day = 6B per day = ~6 * 10K per second = 60K Videos watched/ second
   - Video uploading is less frequent than video watching. Let's assume we have about 1 out of 300 people upload a video. In that case we have about 60K / 300 = 200 Videos per second gets uploaded.
2. **Storage Estimates**
   - Let's say on average each video length is 5 minutes. So we have 200 per second * 5 = 1000 minutes of videos per second. If each minute is about 30 MB size, we have 1000 * 60 MB per second = 30 GB per second.
   - This comes to about 30 * 86.4TB per day = ~2592TB per day = 2.5PB per day raw video.
3. **Bandwidth Estimates**
   - Since video upload and download require a lot of internet bandwidth, let's look at the estimates for the same. With about 30GB storage per second for upload and since our read write ratio is about 300:1, we need to support 30GB + 30 * 300 = ~9TB per second bandwidth support across the system.

So to consolidate, we are dealing with about 60K Video Read requests per second and about 30GB storage per second.

3. API & Model Design

API Design

Our video platform should be able to video viewing and uploading from different devices like TVs, smart phones, tablets etc. So we need to have the backend APIs in REST format so that they can be easily accessible to all the platforms. Let's look at how the APIs need to be defined.

- Object viewVideo(String videoId, String startTime, String resolution, String codec) : this api needs to return the stream of video content at a given startTime, device resolution. Video codec defines the encoding and decoding format of the video for eg: MP4, DivX etc.
- String uploadVideo(String userId, Object videoContent, String title, String description)
- List<String> searchVideo(String searchKey) : Returns list of videoIds.
- String commentVideo(String userId, String videoId, String parentCommentId)

Data Model

Metadata of the users and videos can be maintained in SQL tables. But the actual video object will be stored in a distributed file system that we will see in next sections. Overall SQL Tables can have the following columns.

- User: userId*, userName, creation Time, email, age, passwordHash (Optional salt etc).
- Videos: userId*, ^videoId, title, description, thumbnail Location, size, videoStatus

- VideoStatus indicates if a video is active or inactive or inappropriate

- Comments: *commentId, ^userId, ^videoId, ^parent Comment Id, timestamp, comment.
    - Note that parent CommentId can be used to form conversation threads.

* indicates Primary Key. ^indicates Index key.

Note that the above model is not specific to any database. It represents the overall structure of data.

4. Design & Scalability

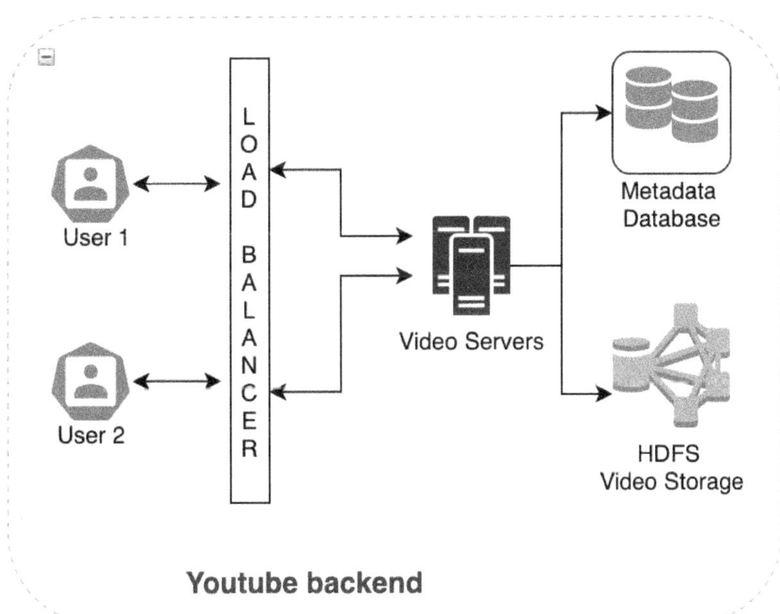

Approach 1 : Basic System design for Youtube

Approach 1: Basic System Design for youtube

Our goal is to build a youtube backend which should primarily allow users to upload videos and view videos. Let's look at a basic approach on how to design this.

- Since we are dealing with millions of users and multiple servers are required to process user requests, we need to have a load balancer in place.
- So all users connect to the load balancer for either view or upload a video. All these requests are directed to video servers which are the main processing app servers.
- When a user uploads a video, video servers save the metadata of the video in the metadata database and the actual video file will be stored in the distributed file storage like HDFS and returns success to the user.
- When a user views the video, the backend video servers read the video from the HDFS storage and send the whole video object to the client viewing the video.

Problems with this approach

Biggest problem with this approach is that it's just not scalable for millions of users as many of the requests need to happen simultaneously. Also sometimes video size can be so big like 5 to 10GB or more. How do we send the whole file efficiently and concurrently to millions of users watching the same video at once? Even though somehow we send the whole blob, the end user client like a browser or mobile app can crash while the video is being rendered to the user.

So let's look at a more scalable approach.

Approach 2: Scalable System Design for Youtube / Netflix

High level diagram

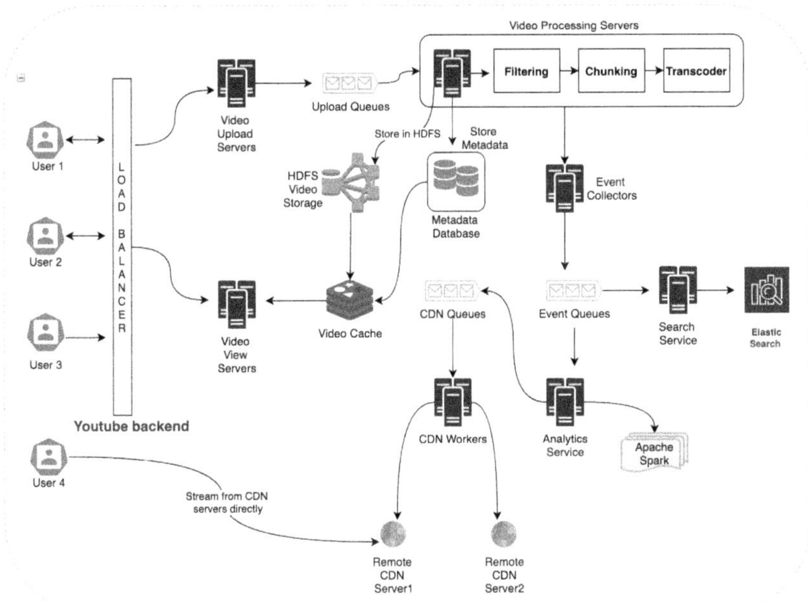

Approach 2 : Scalable System design for Youtube/Netflix

To understand the design for a large scale video system, let's break the problem into individual parts.

Video Upload Flow

In order to handle video uploads, multiple components are involved.

Video Upload Servers

As per our capacity estimations, since we need to handle about 200 video uploads each second, it's important to have a separate cluster of servers dedicated for video uploading. Let's call them *video upload servers.*

- So all the incoming user video uploads are redirected to video upload servers.
- Video upload servers take the whole video file the user has uploaded and store the raw video file in a distributed file storage like HDFS or S3. For our further discussions, let's assume these files are stored in HDFS since it's an open source large scale distributed framework for file storage.
- In addition to it, the video server generates a unique id for the video and saves all the video metadata like title, description, user etc in a sql storage i.e. metadata database.
- Once metadata storage and video storage is successful, the videoId is published as an event into an internal distributed queue for further video processing. Lets name this queue as *Upload Queue*.

Video Processing Workers/Servers

Video processing servers (or workers) are a set of servers which does the actual video processing that involves multiple steps as below.

Video processing servers listen to the 'Upload Queue' for new video uploads. Once an upload event is received, worker server reads the raw video and does various steps as below :

1. Filtering

All the incoming videos need to be checked for any possible system abuse or illegal videos etc. If a video contains inappropriate content the video is marked as inactive in video metadata videoStatus or can be deleted by the system.

2. Chunking

Chunking is a process where a raw video is broken into multiple small pieces. This is required to make sure the video is sent in small parts instead of one big file to someone who views the video.

3. Transcoding

Transcoding is an important step for Adaptive Bitrate Streaming (ABS) for faster video delivery. We will discuss ABS in the immediate section.

As part of transcoding, each video file chunk is converted into various different forms that include

- Different video Codecs like HEVC/H.265, MPEG-4, DivX etc, and different format containers like MP4, AVI, FLV etc in order to support various viewing platforms.
- Different video resolutions like 1080P, 720P, 360P etc. in order to support various screen sizes for TV, mobile, laptop, tablets etc.
- Different Bit rate encoding: In addition to video format, video resolution, each video is optimized for various bandwidth values eg: 1080P/ 5Mbps, 480P/1Mbps etc. This ensures the video is sent faster even for users with small internet bandwidth.

Adaptive Bitrate Streaming (ABS) or Adaptive Video Streaming

Adaptive bitrate streaming (ABS) also called Adaptive video streaming is an amazing technology used to deliver video to a user in the most efficient way possible and in the highest usable quality specific to a given user. When you watch a video on youtube or netflix, you might have observed that the video quality goes higher if our internet speed is good and goes lower if the internet speed is slow right. Similarly if you change the browser window size while the video is playing, the quality might change accordingly. This kind of dynamic switching of video quality and delivery is called adaptive video streaming.

In order to achieve adaptive streaming, as part of the Transcoding step each video is converted into various formats as discussed above. When a user views a video on a client like a browser website or a mobile app, these clients are smart enough to analyze which specific format is best based on the current user viewing constraints. The client evaluates various parameters like internet bandwidth, resolution, video format etc and sends the request to the server with this metadata. This process is continuously evaluated by the client even when the video is playing and the corresponding request is sent to the server while requesting the next chunk of the video. So basically the client switches the video between various formats and conditions and joins various responses and presents to the user. As a quick note, this process of joining and switching back and forth can be called splicing. In order to achieve this level of optimization video bit level data needs to be converted as optimized as possible. Our backend transcoder server converts the uploaded video into various codecs and formats as discussed above and keeps the video ready for viewing. Whenever the client wants to do ABS, it gets the precomputed formats from the backend apis and displays them to the user.

4. Indexing

After the transcoding step, individual chunks and formats are linked together through videoId and chunkId and indexed in the backend file storage. This step ensures speed reads for individual parts when a client requests the video.

Once all the above steps are done, the processed video and the parts are stored in distributed file storage HDFS. Multiple copies of the same video are stored with replication to avoid data loss. After that a video process event is published to the analytics service.

Now let's look at how video viewing works behind the scenes.

Video viewing Flow

As part of the video upload process, each video is thoroughly processed and stored in various chunks and formats for user viewing. This greatly improves the video watching experience. As part of the upload process, each video chunk and formats are stored sequentially on the disk as close as possible for easy disk seeks on the HDFS storage.

When a video request comes for a specific videoId, video watch servers query the video metadata to check the video location and it queries the video storage service to gather various chunks of the video from HDFS and sends the stream of data sequentially to the requesting client.

Above process requires the disk to actually read the video content from the HDFS storage. This process can be a bit slower since it involves physical disk seeks.

In order to improve the speed of video viewing, cache is widely used. Netflix uses EVCache that is built on top of Memcached for caching video content at scale.

Cache

When a video is streamed, chunks of video can be put on cache while the client is streaming. This is like eager loading of data in cache. In addition to it, most frequently accessed videos can be stored in cache for faster viewing.

Since a cache is an in memory storage, if a cache server goes down it means all the data on that server is lost. Since we deal with large amounts of data we need to handle fault tolerance for caches too. To handle this, Netflix has come up with EVCache. EVCache is built on top of Memcached with an additional feature of sharding. When data is loaded into cache, multiple copies of data are stored in sharded nodes with redundancy. So if one machine is down, the data can be retrieved faster from a different cache machine.

SSD Cache

Since RAM is costly compared to disk, maintaining large amounts of video data on an in-memory cache can be expensive in terms of data reloading as well as money expenses. In addition, if multiple copies need to be maintained the cost can further go higher. So SSDs are used by many big companies as an alternative to in-memory caches for some sets of data. In our video storage case, videos that have views not too high and not too low can be put on SSD storage while the high frequent videos can be loaded onto actual cache.

Content Delivery Networks (CDNs)

We know that our videos will be viewed by users across the globe. If we have to minimize video buffering time we need to move the backend video streaming servers as close to the clients as possible. CDNs help solve this problem. If we know a video is most frequently viewed, we can push the video content to different locations in the world. Some services like Netflix set up servers at the locations of internet service providers using the technology called Open Connect. When a user tries to view a video, the user client checks for the nearest CDN location available based on the user location or the ip address origin. Once it resolves the CDN server, it connects to the server and streams the content from that server.

In order to push a video to CDN servers, we need to achieve this in two ways.

1. CDN Push Workers: We can have a set of worker servers which take the file contents of the most frequently watched videos and write the data into remote CDN servers.
2. File Sync with storage: We can setup HDFS or the underlying file storage system to do a data sync for the replicated copy into a remote CDN server.

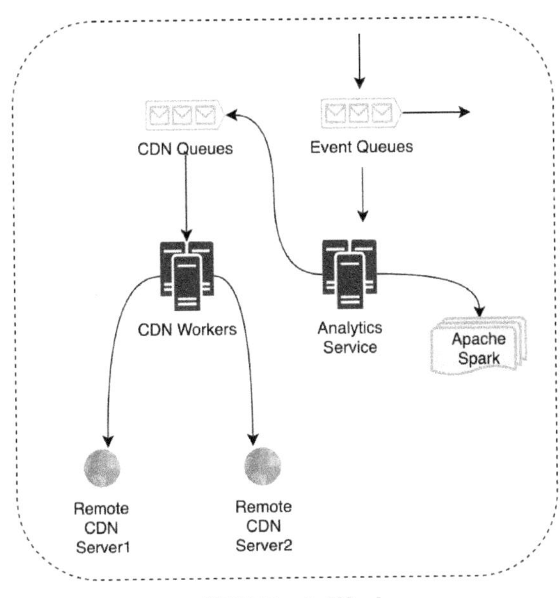

CDN Push Workers

Having CDN sync servers to push content to CDN has more advantages than the other one in our case since we can have more control over which videos to be pushed to which specific locations. Our analytics can indicate some of the data like which videos are most accessed in which countries etc. The workflow can be as below.

As shown in the image above we can have a CDN queue for event processing. Whenever a video is viewed or when a new video is uploaded, the analytics service continuously runs analytics jobs and if it decides a video needs to be pushed, it sends an event to the CDN queue. Set of CDN Sync servers listen to the CDN queue, connect to respective CDN servers and push a copy of processed video content onto the remote CDN server.

Event Processing

Every service in our system produces some kind of event for eg: Video uploaded, video viewed, transcoding completed etc. Since we are dealing with millions of views each second, in order to capture all the events in the system and do asynchronous offline processing, we need to have an Event Collectors service. The primary goal of this service is to serve as a central place to collect all the events across the system, and perform monitoring to our large scale distributed system. It can push data to event queues for offline processing. These event queues can be consumed by various other services like Analytics service, Search service etc.

Netflix uses Apache Chukwa for event collection. Apache Chukwa is an open source data collection system for monitoring large distributed systems. Apache Chukwa is built on top of the Hadoop Distributed File System (HDFS) and Map/Reduce framework and inherits Hadoop's scalability and robustness. Apache Chukwa also includes a flexible and powerful toolkit for displaying, monitoring and analyzing results to make the best use of the collected data.

Analytics

As the service becomes popular, analytics play a key role in taking critical business and system decisions. We need to have an analytics service which listens to all the events in the system through event queues and provides an analytics dashboard and automated workflow systems to initiate critical system workflows. Apache spark can be used for distributed analytics. Apache Spark is an open-source unified analytics engine for large-scale data processing. Spark provides an interface for programming entire clusters with implicit data parallelism and fault tolerance.

Search Service

We should allow users to search for videos in our system. To do that, every video that gets uploaded needs to be indexed for search based on title, description at the minimum. Some more advanced features like searching subtitles, search based on video thumbnails etc can be indexed as required. We can use ElasticSearch for video search indexing. Elasticsearch is a distributed, free and open search and analytics engine for all types of data, including textual, numerical, geospatial, structured, and unstructured. Elasticsearch is built on Apache Lucene and was first released in 2010 by Elasticsearch N.V. (now known as Elastic). Known for its simple REST APIs, distributed nature, speed, and scalability, Elasticsearch is the central component of the Elastic Stack, a set of free and open tools for data ingestion, enrichment, storage, analysis, and visualization. Commonly referred to as the ELK Stack (after Elasticsearch, Logstash, and Kibana), the Elastic Stack now includes a rich collection of lightweight shipping agents known as Beats for sending data to Elasticsearch. Elasticsearch is widely used by various companies to do search indexing. Alternatively we can build our own search engine with more customizations to do the video search.

5. Final Thoughts and Future Extensibility

As we saw in the previous section, the scalable system design works well for most use cases. Now, if you want to scale it further to the next level what components can we optimize ? Let's dive in.

Fault Tolerance and latency across systems

We have a lot of distributed components across the system. What if one of the components goes down ? How can we make sure we have fallbacks to backup storage ? To do that we need to have latency management and fault tolerant libraries plugged into our code at each layer. Hystrix, resilience4j and Sentinal are good examples for fault tolerant libraries. To understand more on this consider the below scenario.

Let's say a video upload server is writing a raw video file to the HDFS cluster. Suddenly if there is a network partition due to internet outage for one of the internal networks. Then we need to fallback the file writing to either a different storage or to a local disk in order to continue serving users right. If we have to do this kind of switching between network connections in our application code, it becomes a maintenance nightmare to do multiple switches across multiple components. To solve this we can have fault tolerant libraries like Hystrix, resilience4j which are specifically designed for handling these scenarios. So once you plugin hystrix/resilience4j into the code, you can control the fallbacks and http connection latencies with dynamic configurations. Netflix uses Hystrix for this. They have recently migrated to resilience4j inorder to achieve Adaptive concurrent limits. Features like CircuitBreaker, Rate Limiter, Fallback etc can be controlled at scale with reslience4j as discussed in the "Fault Tolerance" section of this book.

Stateless MicroServices

As discussed before, dealing with million requests per second requires optimizations at each individual component level. If we have to do that, it's better to separate the resources based on the type of services they offer eg: search service, analytics service etc. So youtube or netflix uses lots of microservices (Refer to *Monolithic vs Microservices* section for more details) with each service serving a specific purpose. In our Approach2, we saw that video processing servers do multiple steps like transcoding, chunking etc. To have a system at scale since each of these steps are time consuming processes, instead of having them grouped into a single service we can further divide them into micro services. The design can look like below.

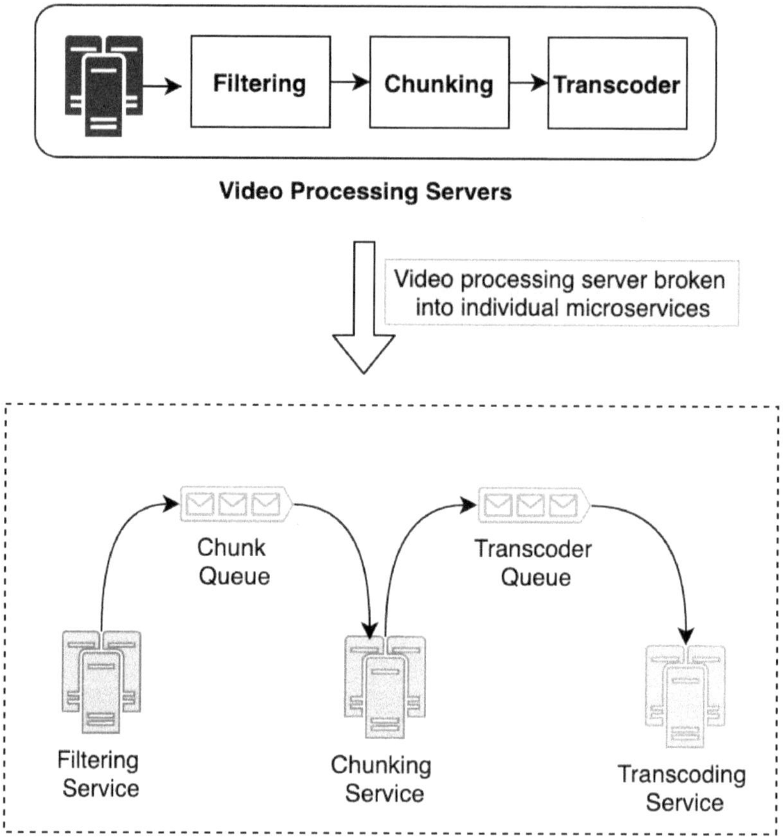

Microservices for each action

Each core action like filtering, chunking, transcoder can be broken into individual microservices. Each of these services can interact with each other with a service queue. So the Filter service passes the message to the chunk queue. Chunking service listens to the chunk queue and performs the video chunking process for the queue message received and this process can continue. In this way each service can be individually maintained and scaled as required.

Since the servers in each of the microservices can fail at any time, it's important to keep these servers stateless i.e required app data can be recovered from one of the storage instances and configurations should be dynamic. Zookeeper can be used for distributed coordination and coordination across these microservices.

Application Gateway

So far we discussed all the internals of the system. There are other aspects of the system such as dynamic request routing, security, user authentication and various other aspects. Our service can be used by multiple users from various platforms like mobiles, tablets, laptops etc. So it's important to have a common gateway which can access the incoming requests originating from these devices and adding orthogonal functionalities and request filters for each of the requests.

Netflix uses ZUUL as a front door to do this. ZUUL is an L7 application gateway front door for all requests from devices and web sites to thc backend of the Netflix streaming application. As an edge service application, Zuul is built to enable dynamic routing, monitoring, resilience and security. It also has the ability to route requests to multiple Amazon Auto Scaling Groups as appropriate.Similar to ZUUL we can configure application gateways for our app frontend to handle the user requests.

As discussed in all the above sections, we can extend our application at each of the levels. Video streaming is definitely one of the challenging applications to scale. Think through various use cases on top of what we discussed here and try to plugin those use cases into our design. Discuss with your interviewer for specific use cases and play around the topics that we covered. This should keep you in a good position for system design interviews.

References

https://netflixtechblog.com/high-quality-video-encoding-at-scale-d159db052746

https://youtube-eng.googleblog.com/2018/04/making-high-quality-video-efficient.html

https://www.youtube.com/watch?v=UklDSMG9ffU&t=846s

https://github.com/resilience4j/resilience4j#overview

Chapter 8

Must Learn Important Interview Question 5

Design Yelp or Foursquare or Nearby Friends

1. Introduction & Requirement Analysis

The next important interview question every one must learn is how to design location based search applications like Yelp, Foursquare or Google reviews location search etc. Let's try to understand the use case.

Yelp is a crowd-sourced local business review and social networking site. One of the main features of yelp is the location based search. Let's say you want to know what are the top restaurants that are near to you within 10 miles. You can use yelp to search for this. If we are asked to design a service like yelp in a system design interview, how can we do it ? Let's dive in. First let's settle on specific requirements that we cover as part of our design.

Functional Requirements

1. Users should be able to search for places within a given distance.

2. Users can filter places by parameters like rating, cost of service etc.
3. Restaurant or business owners should be able to add or remove new places
4. Users should be able to provide ratings for the places like 1 to 5 starts.
5. Users can add comments and upload images to individual places.

Non Functional Requirements

1. System should be highly available and accurate: User search results should be as accurate as possible for the given distance and filters.
2. System has more reads compared to writes: Adding new places is relatively less frequent than searching for places.
3. System should be highly reliable: Places should not be lost while indexing or in any instance.

2. Capacity estimations

Let's say our system has about 1 Billion places across the globe. Let the daily active users be 100 Million. Since the number of places added into the system are relatively less compared to number of searches users make, let the read to write ratio be 100:1

With the above numbers, let's calculate QPS and Storage estimates.

1. **Requests Per second:**
    - Let's say each user does 10 searches per day. So we have 200 Million daily users * 10 = 2B searches per day = 1000M / 86400 = 10 * 2000K/ 864 = ~20K / second.
2. **Storage Estimates:**
    - If we consider each place table entry takes roughly 1MB storage then for 1Billion places we need 1B * 1MB = 1PB of storage. For 5 years we need 5PB of storage

3. API & Model Design

API Design

Now let's formalize the requirements with the API design

- Search for places:
    - JSON search(String query, Long distance) : returns JSON results of places
- Filter results:
    - JSON search(String query, Long distance, FilterType[] filters, FilterValue[] values) : Returns search results by applying respective filter types and filter valucs.
- Add Place:
    - String addPlace(Place place) : returns PlaceId after adding new place
- Edit Place:
    - Boolean editPlace(String placeId, Place place) : returns true if edit is success and false if edit is failure.

- Rate a place:
  - Void ratePlace(String placeId, int rating) : rating indicates number between 1 to 5.
- Comment Place:
  - String comment(String comment, Object media) : Optional comment text, Media object for image or videos.

Model Design

For model design, we will initially list all the model tables for metadata. For storing places search index we will use a different format that we will discuss in the design section. Let's look at model design for Yelp metadata.

Since we are dealing with about 1 Billion places, we can store the data in NoSQL or SQL tables.

SQL Tables:

The sql format of metadata is as follows:

- Users: userId*, userName, creation Time, email, age, password Hash (Optional salt etc).
- Places: *placeId, title, description, openhours, address, ^latitude, ^longitude, category, media Location
- Comments: *commentId, ^userId, ^placeId, parent CommentId, timestamp, comment, media Location.
  - Note that parent CommentId can be used to form conversation threads.
- Ratings: ^placeId, ^userId, rating

NoSQL Table structure.

Core tables like Places, Comments can be stored in NoSQL format to accommodate future scaling.

- Places:
  - rowKey: placeId
  - columnKey: Constant (A fixed value for all the keys)
  - columnValue: PlaceObject
    - PlaceObject can have multiple attributes like the attributes shown in SQL Places table.
- Comments: Since we load comments for a particular place, we can have the following structure.
  - rowKey : placeId
  - columnKey : timestamp
  - columnValue: CommentObject.
    - CommentObject can have attributes similar to Comments SQL tables as keyvalues.
  - When a place is loaded, we query this table to get a list of all comments sorted by timestamp and display the results to the user. Adding a new comment will palace an entry in this table

* indicates PrimaryKey. ^ indicates index key.

4. Design & Scalability

The trickiest part of Yelp's nearby location system design is "How can we get a list of places within a given distance". This kind of search by location is also called *proximity search.* Before jumping into proximity search, first let's see how our overall components interact with each other.

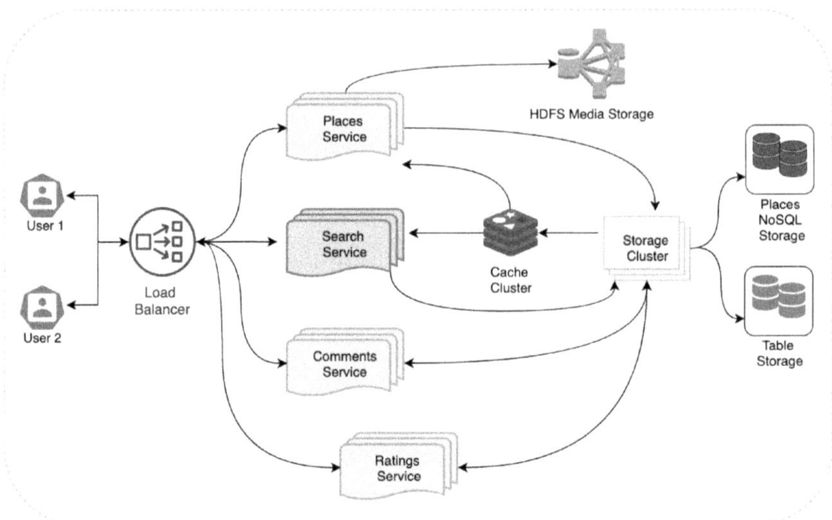

System design for Yelp Nearby Search

When a user tries to access our website, depending on the type of action, the request will be routed to one of the four services as shown in the image above.

1. **Places Service:** Whenever a user tries to add or delete or update a place, the request is routed to places service. Places service is backed by three components.
    - Storage Cluster: Storage cluster comprises NoSQL storage and SQL Storage. Since we are dealing with more than a billion places in our system, for storing the places we can use the NoSQL storage. The NoSQL places storage is as per the schema mentioned in the Data Model section of this chapter.
    - HDFS Storage: Every place can have a place image associated with the place. This image is stored in the HDFS storage and the location is saved along with the places table.

- Cache Cluster: Since places are the most frequently used data, we can cache the placeId, PlaceOject data in cache for faster reads.

2. **Search Service:** This is the main and most complicated service which retrieves the list of all the places based on the search query, search filters and location based searches. We will discuss this in detail in a few moments.

3. **Comments Service:** Whenever someone visits a place and wants to comment on a specific location, the respective requests come to this service. Comments service is driven by MySQL storage or NoSQL storage. Since we are dealing with about 1 Billion places and each place can have multiple comments, storing in NoSQL can give a good scaling factor. Each comment can have following attributes

   Comments: *commentId, ^userId, ^placeId, parent CommentId, timestamp, comment, mediaLocation.

   All the attributes look straight forward except the *parentCommentId* field. *parentCommentId* can be used to form conversation threads between comments. Let's say we have a user who comments on a place. If some other user replies to the above comment specifically then we can store the parent comment in the parentCommentId and the respective thread can be rendered in the UI.

4. **Ratings Service:** Similar to comments service, ratings service keeps track of ratings of a specific place. Rating can vary between 1 to 5. Every time a user provides a rating, it can calculate the rating of a restaurant. Rating calculation can be very simple logic like average rating of all the users or can have much complex logic. For example depending

on the user rating we can bring in a weight factor for rating from a specific user to a specific place. This helps in avoiding abuse of the rating system.

Search By Location

Now that we know what services mainly our system should have, let's get into the crux of the Proximity Search problem i.e. If we want to provide a list of places within a certain distance of the user's current location, how can we achieve it efficiently ?

To explain this, let's take an example search.

Let's say we have a user who is searching for a list of all the restaurants within 10 miles of his current location. How can we achieve that ?

Approach 1: SQL Based Approach

In our design we considered the factor that each place can be stored in a SQL system too. Each place can have a attributes like

Places: *placeId, title, description, openhours, address, ^latitude, ^longitude, ^category, mediaLocation

If you look at the above table structure every place has a latitude and longitude. When a user performs a search from a specific location, we can collect the latitude and longitude information from the GPS coordinates of the user through our app or website. Also if the user is interested in specific categories, say restaurants,we can get the categoryId either from the cache of an Enum kind of variable for a category since there would be a handful of categories. Since we have user as well as restaurant/ place latitude and longitude information, we can write an SQL query like below :

Let user latitude, longitude coordinates be (X, Y). Let the distance within which he wants to search be 'C'. Category of restaurants be 'R'

Approximate SQL Query can be :

*SELECT * FROM Places WHERE latitude BETWEEN (X - C, X + C) AND longitude BETWEEN (Y - C, Y + C) AND category = 'R'*

From the above query we are getting all the places with latitude and longitude in the range of distance of the user location. This query is not very accurate because it doesn't exactly cover the radius.

On top of the above query, we still have to apply search filters like restaurant title, description etc. So if we have to rely on sql, we might have to use a "LIKE" kind of query to search within the text which may not be very efficient.

But the scale of our system is very high. We have about 1billion places in the Places table. Even though latitude, longitude columns are indexed it still takes a long time to scan through the index and perform intersection. Dealing with 20K Queries per second with the above query is not scalable.

So instead of this approach, let's look at a different approach.

Approach 2: Static Grids

When we look at the previous approach, we are trying to search across various locations that we have in the system through index and on top of it we might have to apply other search filters. These places can be present anywhere in the world.

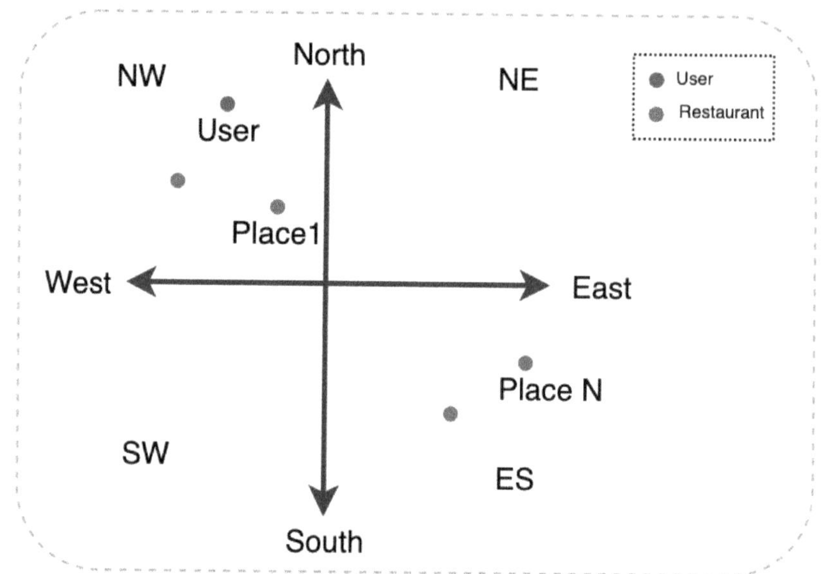

User , Restaurants Distrubution

When the places are scattered across the globe, what is the point of searching them when they are far away from where the user is located ? As shown in image above, if a user is in a North west location of the globe and a restaurant Place N is in a East South coordinate, then there is no point of searching through that location if the user wants a location within 10 miles distance right!

So we need to somehow narrow down the number of places that we need to search. To do this, we can divide the whole world into individual grids (or segments or mathematically similar to quadrants). Like in the above image whole world can be divided into 4 grids i.e. NW, NE, ES, SW. So if a user is searching for a location in the NW grid then we can confine our search for locations only within that quadrant and skip search through the rest of the three grids.

This reduces our search space into 1/4th. If we can apply the same logic and divide a grid into much smaller grids it will further reduce our search space. So the whole earth can be divided into individual smaller grids in the shape of a square with the length of each side being of some constant value, say 'L'.

So the resultant geographical map divided into smaller grids looks like below.

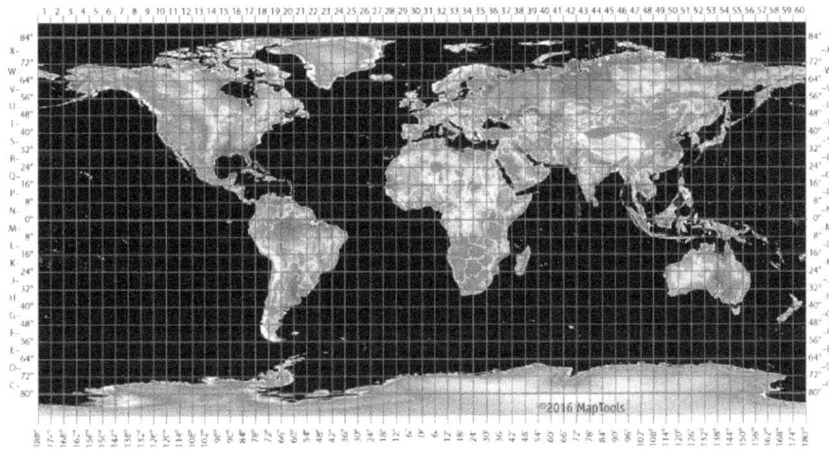

(Source: https://www.maptools.com/tutorials/grid_zone_details)

Above image gives a very good picture of how earth is divided into individual smaller grids.

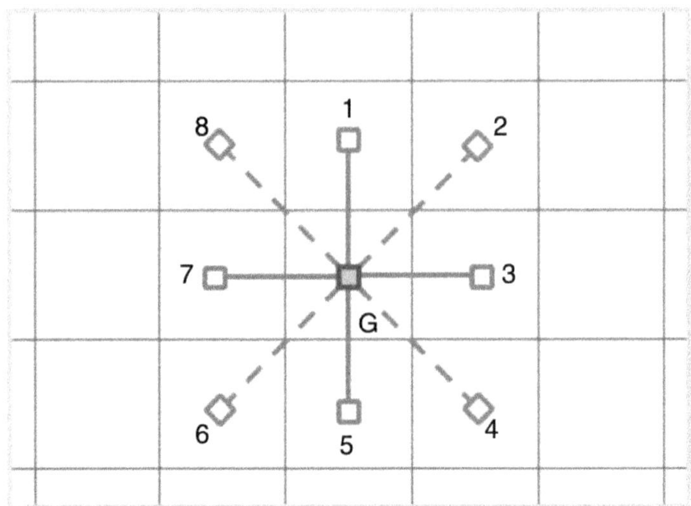

Distances from center to neighbour grids

(Source: https://eng.uber.com/h3/)

What should be the ideal length of each side i.e. the value of 'L' ? Typically if we query mostly in the surrounding area of 10 miles then the grid side length can be 10 miles. The reason being we can confine the most frequent searches to a single grid length and its neighboring grids. So if a user is present in grid 'G', then if we search the surrounding 8 grids i.e. 1 to 8 then we can guarantee that we can retrieve all the relevant places in the nearest location possible with these 8 grids.

Each grid will have a gridId. During the grid allocation process, we need to keep track of which specific grid a latitude and longitude belongs to. So each place can have an additional parameter of gridId in the storage. Updated Places and Grid tables schema is as follows:

- Places: *placeId, title, description, openhours, address, ^latitude, ^longitude, category, mediaLocation, ^gridId
- Grid: *gridId, x1,x2,y1,y2
  - Where (x1, y1) represent the bottom left point of the grid and (x2, y2) represent the top right corner of the grid.

How to get gridId of current location?

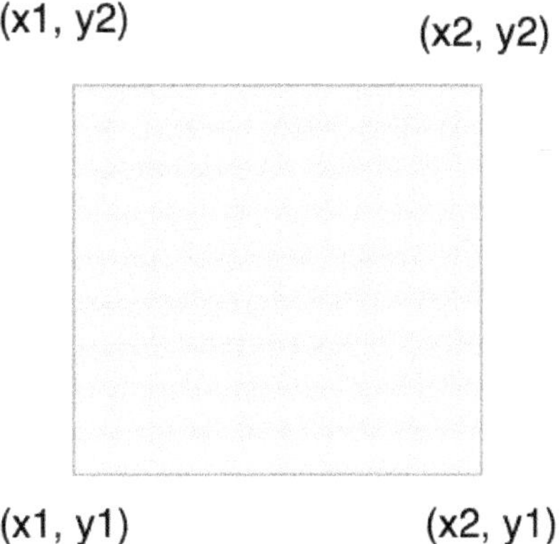

Grid Coordinates for each corner

In our grid table we store coordinates of the bottom left corner and top right corner i.e. (x1,y1) and (x2,y2). So if a new point is given (a,b) if it has to be present inside this grid, then we need to apply a mathematical formula to check if a point is present inside the rectangle or not.

If x1 <= a <= x2 AND y1 <= b <= y2 then we can say a point is present inside the grid. So we can query the grid table as follows.

SELECT gridId from Grids WHERE x1 <= a AND a <= x2 AND y1 <= b AND b <= y2.

There should be a single gridId which matches this condition and that result is returned as the gridId of the current location.

How to search for the nearest places ?

From the above step, we can get the gridId of the current location. From that we can get the gridIds of the neighboring locations by calculating the coordinates of each of the grids using the distance range and the current location. Let's say the coordinates of each of the 8 grids are gridA, gridB and so to gridH.

Using this we get all the places that belong to these 8 gridIds in addition to the gridId of the current location. The query looks like below:

Search Query

*SELECT * FROM Places WHERE latitude between X-10 and X+10 and Longitude between Y-10 and Y+10 and GridID in (currentGridId, gridA, gridB, ... gridH) AND category = 'R'.*

Since we can have gridId as an index and also the category filter is already applied, the number of places that are returned can be very fast and overall the query performance is widely improved compared to approach 1.

Problems with this approach:

This approach works totally fine if the number of places per grid are equally distributed. But in the real world this is not the case. Populated cities like Los Angeles are denser than some remote areas. So dealing with a large number of places within the same grid size could be a problem as we grow. To solve this, let's look at a dynamic grids approach.

Approach 3: Dynamic Grids

In Approach 2, we assumed the size of each grid is constant. So if we can make the size of the grid dynamic based on the number of places that are present in the grid then we can avoid the above mentioned problem. So while allocating grids, if we find that a grid reaches a certain threshold amount of places, then we need to further divide the grid into much smaller grids. But since the grid size became complex, the way we need to represent the grid and query the grid becomes complex. To address the storage of dynamic grids we can rely on a data structure called **QuadTree**

QuadTree

A QuadTree is a tree data structure in which each internal node has exactly four children. In our case, as we allocate grids for each geographical area, if we find a grid has more locations than our threshold, we will divide the grid into four more subgrids. As shown in the figure below, let 'A' be the current grid. As we detect more density, A can be further divided into four more subgrids A1, A2, A3, A4. Observe the color differences for each of the grids. This is the first level of partition. If we find thc subgrid A2 has many morc placcs than our threshold we can divide it further into smaller subgrids A2_1, A2_2, A2_3, A3_4.

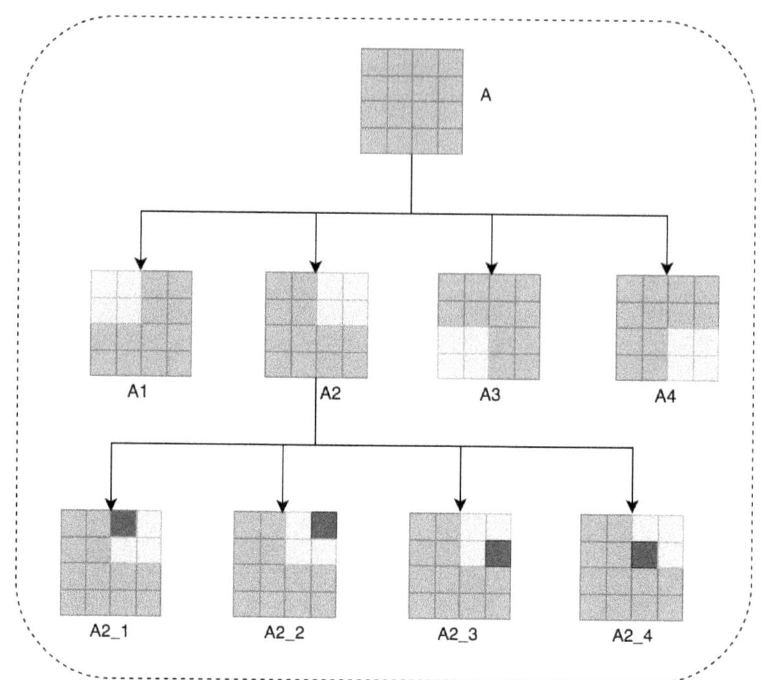

QuadTree representation for Location Grids of Earth

QuadTree can support the above representation of grids. Size of each grid becomes one fourth for every tree level. To build a quadtree like above assume that our threshold C to be 1000 places per grid.

- Consider the whole earth as one big grid, the root node.
- We will start with the root node and since this grid A has places count > C, we can divide this into 4 subgrids and add them as children to the root node.
- Now for each of the children we will check for the threshold. If the places count > C then we will recursively divide each of these into smaller grids and finally we can achieve the above QuadTree.

New Place Insertion

We now know how to create the QuadTree. If we have to insert a new place into our grid system,we will need to find the grid for which this place belongs. (We will discuss this in the next section i.e. 'Find the grid for location' section). Once we know the gridId, we can insert the place in this grid. Now let's say the number of places in the specific grid crossed the threshold after inserting the new place. In that case we need to split the current grid into smaller grids similar to the steps in the previous section.

Find the grid for a location

Typical way to find the specific grid of a location is to do a DFS (depth first search). Steps are as follows.

- Start with the root node.
- Check the 4 children to detect if the user location is in the range of grid coordinate range.
- Out of the 4 children, we will get one grid which has the range of user location.
- Now go to that grid and recursively perform step 2 until a final leaf node is reached.

You can think of it like doing a search in a Binary Search tree. The difference is instead of checking 2 child nodes we will check 4 nodes and the coordinate ranges.

Let's call this as the currentUserGridId.

How to search for the places within the user range

In order to search for places, we need to know the currentUserGridId of the current user location as well the gridIds of the neighboring node locations. We know currentUserGridId from the previous step. Now we need to know the gridIds of the neighboring grids. Since each grid is subdivided into 4 subgrids, neighboring nodes are just siblings to each other. Front the currentUserGridId neighboring grids are nothing but the siblings of the parent node. To get the parent node from the current node the simplest way to achieve that is to maintain a pointer to a parent for every node. So from the current node, go to the parent, then go to the grand parent and get all the children. In that way we can get the siblings of the parents.

Once we get all the neighboring grids, we can apply the query that we saw in the "Search Query" of "Approach 2. Static Grids: " section to retrieve the nearby places.

How to store QuadTree?

We saw that QuadTree is a good data structure to store our grid data. We can store the QuadTree in memory backed by a disk. When we store the QuadTree in memory, does it fit in a single machine ? Probably not, because we are dealing with billions of places and a large number of grids. So we need to divide the QuadTree into partitions and load it into memory and serve the requests. Whenever there is a change in QuadTree structure we can persist that to the disk, so that if a specific quadtree server dies, we can recover it from the disk. How can we partition the quadtree data ?

Partition By Region

If we can keep the grids that are close by in one single partition that will greatly improve the performance of the system because for most queries we can hit just one server to read the nearby grids. So one way to partition the QuadTree is to divide the nodes based on the regions, say a postal code or a district code etc. But then if a region has more places we will go back to our original problem of creating hot grids.

Partition By Location

We can apply consistent hashing to our problem. Each place that is present in our system can have a unique PlaceId. Based on this placeId we can apply consistent hashing so that it's easier to redistribute the data as well as perform easier lookups.

But since it's hash based, all the nearby grids may not be in a single server. So we need to have a separate process which accumulates all the data from various servers and does the final search queries.

Even though this approach involves querying more servers, this can be a more reasonable approach compared to the first one since we can scale the system horizontally by adding more servers.

Putting this all together, the final design looks like below.

We will have a separate service called GridService. This service manages all the activities related to Grid creation, modifications etc. This grid service queries the underlying QuadTree servers to get the data from the QuadTree index and returns the grid specific information to the clients.

Grid Service also manages the rebalancing of QuadTree when a place is added or deleted from the system. The diagram looks like below.

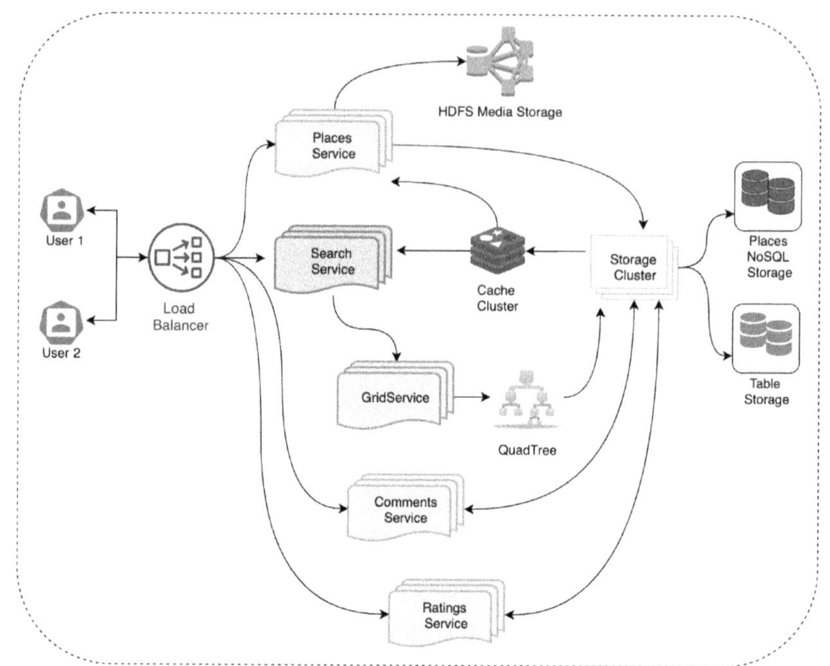

System design for Yelp with QuadTree

5. Final Thoughts and Future Extensibility

We have seen the system design based on the QuadTree structure. Given the scale of service with billions of places there is definitely scope to improve. Let's look at various aspects.

Caching

One of the primary ways we can speed up our application is to leverage the use of Cache. When a user queries for places nearby, the location vs gridId mapping data can be cached. Similarly ratings of a place can be cached because it rarely changes data. Place comments can be cached. Whenever the places service, comments service, ratings service, search service hits the backend storage, we can place the most frequently used data in the cache cluster so that they can be used during the read calls. Redis or memcached can be used for in memory caching.

Replication

We are dealing with multiple servers for the storage of QuadTree structure. Each search has a certain amount of data for a QuadTree. What if one of the servers has a failed hard disk or some kind of hardware failure. There could be a chance that the data can be lost. To avoid this we need to maintain replication for the servers. Each server can have a master slave setup for the data. Whenever the data in master changes it gets synced with the slave. When the master fails, we can switch over the server to the slave server.

Filters

So far we have seen the design for getting places near by to the user. If we want to support additional filters on top of the location filter what can we do ? We can achieve this in two ways.

1. Get all the Places based on the location and then apply the list of filters on top of the result set. This way the we don't tend to miss the places
2. Second method is to add the filter attributes as part of the search query. This method increases the query filtering time. To achieve maximum efficiency for this, we need to properly index all the filter types

Grid shape

We have seen that QuadTree is used to solve the search query. Why should we divide the earth only into rectangular shapes i.e. into 4 grids for each node? Why not some other shape say a triangle or a hexagon or something else ?

Car booking company - Uber did an extensive research for this to handle the real time drive matching location algorithm. They found that hexagon is the best fit for the geographical grid partition.

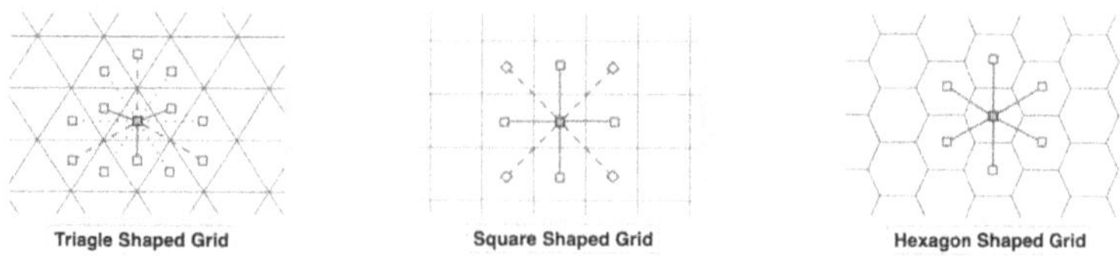

Neighbour grid representation for Triangle, Square, Hexagon

As you can see in the image above, each of the three shapes viz. Triangle, Square, Hexagon shaped grid partitions are compared. If the grid is shaped in the form of a triangle each grid will have 12 neighbour grids. Square has 8 neighbour grids. But for hexagon it has just 6 neighbours distributed equally. As you can see Hexagon is much better in shape to query since it involves the least amount of grids while covering the places efficiently. So hexagon can be chosen for our location based search too.

H3 is a geospatial indexing system developed by Uber using a hexagonal grid that can be (approximately) subdivided into finer and finer hexagonal grids, combining the benefits of a hexagonal grid with S2's hierarchical subdivisions. Wide usage of H3 library can be seen in the Uber system design.

References

https://eng.uber.com/h3/

https://www.youtube.com/watch?v=ay2uwtRO3QE

Chapter 9

Must Learn Important Interview Question 6

Design Search AutoSuggestions

1. Introduction & Requirement Analysis

Predictiction is one of the greatest innovations of technology.

Search engines have become so smart that when you start typing something that you want to search, they actually try to give auto suggestions on what you are typing too. On a funny note, they just make us lazy even to type something :-). Did you ever wonder how these autocomplete predictions pop up when you search ? In this chapter we are going to discuss the system design of how auto suggestions can work at scale.

Let's take the below example. The moment you start typing 'wh' in google, you see a set of suggestions like ['whole foods', 'whatsapp', ... etc]. Since 'wh' is the beginning of the sentence it's called prefix. To design a system like this, let's jump into the requirements.

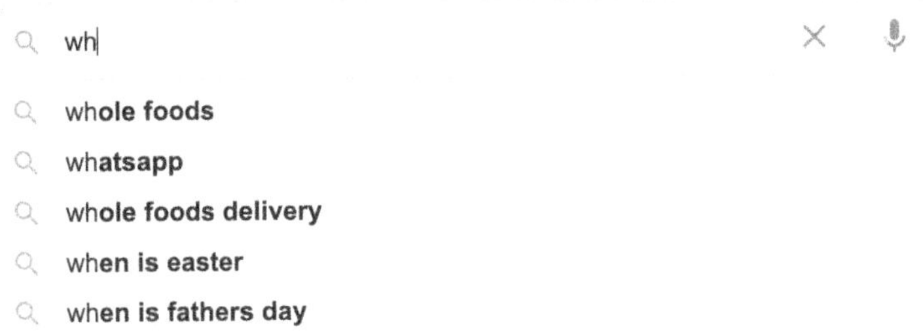

wh

whole foods
whatsapp
whole foods delivery
when is easter
when is fathers day

Functional Requirements

1. Users should be able to get a list of suggestions for a given search prefix.
2. Every time the prefix changes, the suggestions can change as per the modified prefix.
3. Auto suggestions should be based on the frequently searched queries.

Non Functional Requirements

1. Suggestions should be instant. System should have minimum latency.
2. System should be highly available.
3. System can be eventually consistent i.e. if a new query is added into the system, its ok if two different users have some delay in having updated query suggestions.

Optional Additional Requirements

1. Query suggestions need to be filtered for abusive keywords.
2. User search history can be to be part of the suggested sentences.

2. Capacity estimations

Google processes roughly about 4 billion searches per day as of 2021 (Source: internetlivestats.com). Let's say on average each search query has 5 keywords with each word about 5 characters each, we have 5 * 5 = 25characters per search.

1. **Requests Per second**
    - So for a volume of 4B searches each day if we have to roughly provide suggestions for 80% of the queries, we have 4B * 25 * 0.8 = 8B autosuggestion queries per day since we need to provide suggestions for each character for 80% of the queries.
    - So 8B per day = ~10K * 8 = ~80K Requests per second. (Refer cheat sheet for approximation)
2. **Storage Estimates**
    - For storage, since each query is about 25 characters we need about 25 bytes for storing an average query.
    - Out of the 4B search queries, there will be a lot of duplicates. If we assume 25% of the queries are new ones and if we index top 20% of the search terms, then we will have 4B * 0.25 * 0.2 = 200 Million queries.
    - So to store 200 Million queries, we need 200M * 25 bytes = 5GB of new storage space per day.

3. API & Model Design

API Design

Let's see what the APIs look like.

- For getting auto suggestions
    - List<String> getSuggestions(String prefix) : returns list of strings for autosuggestion.
- Add suggestion
    - Void addSuggestion(String term) : Adds auto suggestion into the system.

Model Design

Before jumping into the model design, it's important to understand how auto suggestions need to be stored. To understand this we will look at the high level design and discuss the storage model as we progress.

4. Design & Scalability

Let's look at how we can get the list of suggestions for a given prefix and how to design the end to end system.

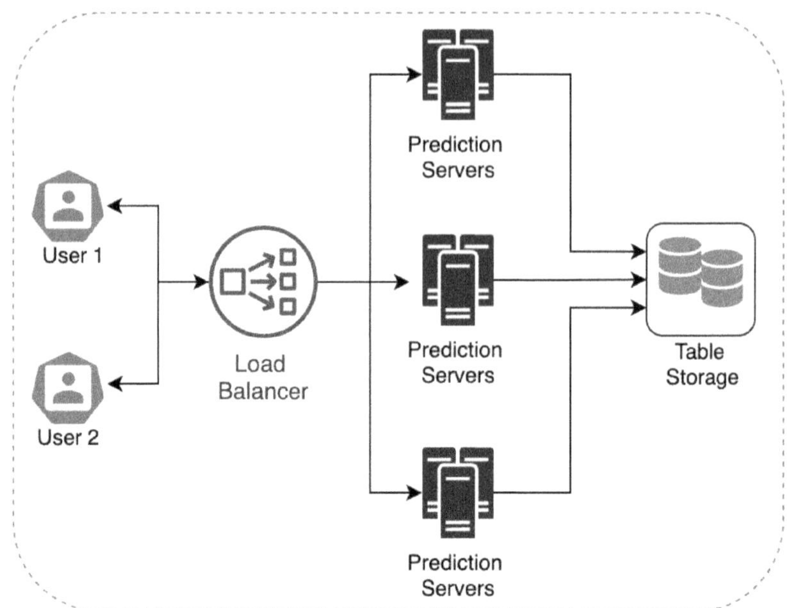

Naive System design for Search Auto suggestions

Approach 1: Naive Approach

If our search queries count is low we can have a system like above.

- When a user starts typing a query in the search bar, for every character a Http request can be sent to the backend system like shown above.
- Each request lands on a load balancer. Load balancer directs the request to one of the Prediction servers.
- We can store all the search queries that our system has in the form of an SQL Table (say Queries table). For the given prefix say a variable named 'prefix' (in our example prefix = 'wh'), we can run a sql query like below:

* *SELECT * FROM Queries WHERE sentence LIKE 'prefix%' LIMIT 10*

- Prediction servers get the results and give the response to the incoming user request.

Problems with this approach

When the number of total search terms in our system are less, then the above approach might work. But we are designing the system at a scale of about 80K requests per second. Also the search terms are about millions of rows. Doing a LIKE SQL query has a lot of performance issues when we are dealing with millions of rows. Overall system is not scalable with this approach.

Approach 2: Tries

Let's look at a more efficient approach. Before jumping into the end to end design of our system we need to find a way to efficiently retrieve the auto suggestions. Consider the below example,

Reference Example

Input Prefix: wh

Relevant sentences can be :

"whole foods"

"whole foods delivery"

"whatsapp"

"when is easter"

"when is fathers day"

If we observe the above sentences that are relevant to each other, the prefixes of each of the sentences are related to each other. So if we can group the sentences by prefix and form some kind of a tree where each child belongs to a specific prefix that can save us a lot of space. Also since it's like a tree format we can do a Depth first search (DFS) to retrieve the data right ? Going in these lines, the most suited data structure to store auto suggestions data is a **"Trie"**

NOTE: If you are familiar with Trie, you can skip the "What is a Trie" section and go directly into the "Auto Suggestion" section.

What is a Trie?

Trie (also called as prefix tree) is a kind of search tree, where each node holds

1. A map of all the children with key : Next character, Value: Next character's node. Reason that children are mapped as map is that the lookup can be faster using the starting character instead of a list.
2. A boolean whether the current node is a leaf or not.

```
class TrieNode {
    Map<Character, TrieNode> childMap;
    boolean amILeaf;
}
```

An example of Trie is shown below.

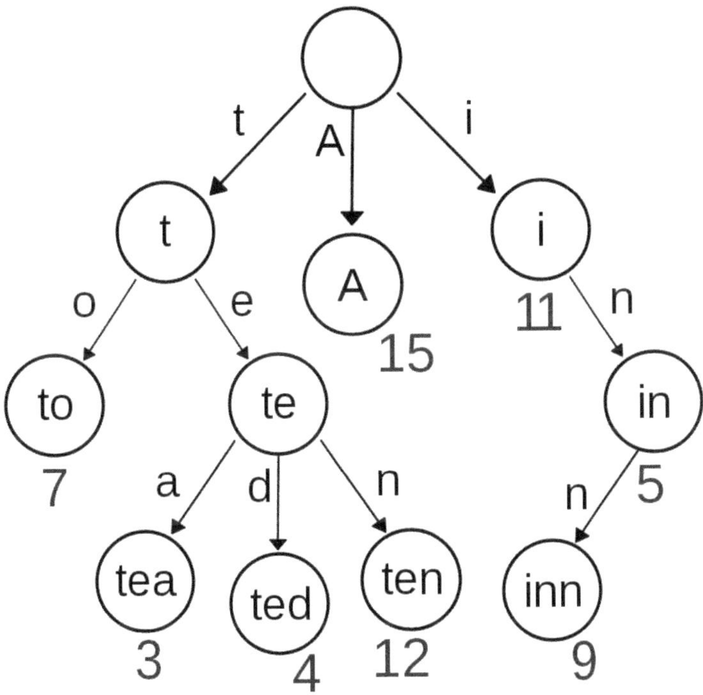

(Source: Wikipedia)

Above diagram represents a trie for keys "A", "to", "tea", "ted", "ten", "i", "in", and "inn". Each leaf node represents one complete word. Every non leaf node has a list of children for each of which the current node is a prefix. Eg: Node "te" has three children "tea", "ted", "ten". Since "te" is the common prefix for all the three words, node "te" has three children.

For the words "what", "whatsapp", "whole", "whole foods", "demo" trie can be represented as shown below

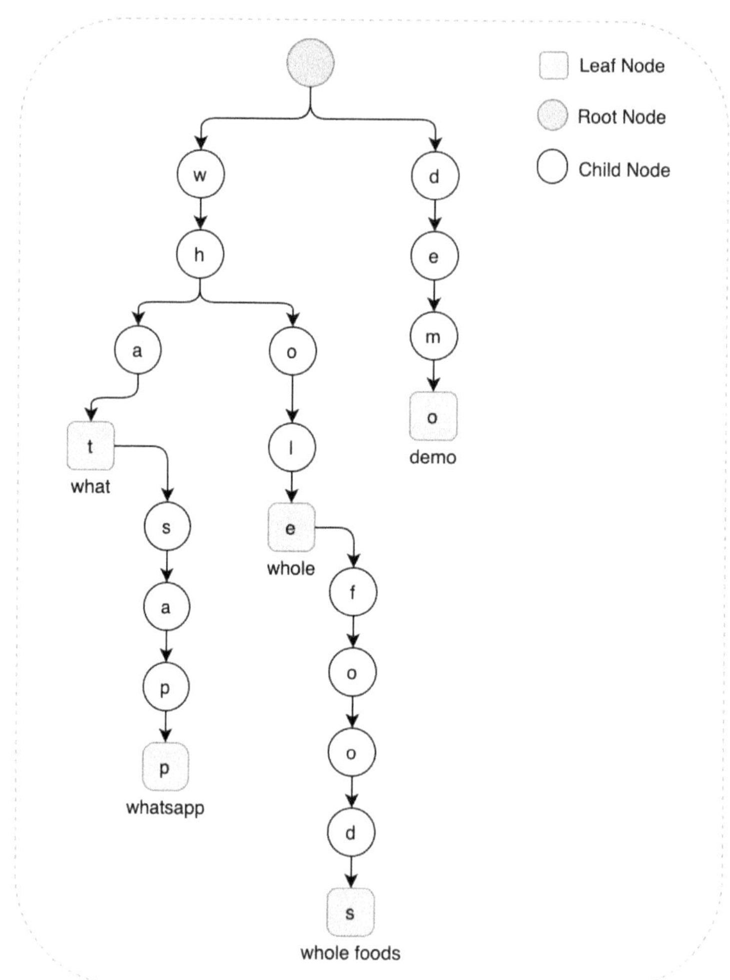

Trie representation for (what, whatsapp, whole, whole foods, demo)

Root nodes in a trie are always empty. So the root node in the picture above is empty. Each node can have multiple children with each child representing a unique character. As we can see from the trie representation, since all the sample words start with the letters 'w' or 'd', the root node has two children with

Node('w') and Node['d']. Node 'w' has one child node 'h' since all the words start with 'wh'. Node('h') has two children nodes Node ('a') and Node('o') because the words can be started with 'wha' or 'who'. Similarly words starting with 'wha' have 't' as the next character. So only Node('t') is the child of Node('a').. As we reach Node('t'), we see that 'what' is actually part of the sample word list. So Node ('t') is marked as leaf node with the boolean variable amILeaf as true (indicated in rounded rectangle in above diagram). Also Node('t') has one possible next character as 's' from the word ('whatsapp'). So it has one child Node ('s') and the whole structure continues until all the words are covered as part of the leaf nodes. Note that we use the terminology of leaf nodes to represent a full word. Please don't get confused with a regular tree leaf node where it doesn't have any children. For the above trie each of the leaf nodes represent full terms like 'demo', 'what', 'whatsapp' etc.

Construction/Insertion of Nodes: We construct the Trie by iterating each of the input words one by one. Each character of the input word is taken and the relationships are formed. For the sample list : "what", "whatsapp", "whole", "whole foods", "demo". Each word is iterated and inserted into the trie with the below code.

```
class TrieNode {
    Map<Character, TrieNode> childMap;
    boolean amILeaf;
}

/** Inserts a word into the trie. */
public void insert(TrieNode root, String word) {

    TrieNode node = root;
    for(char w : word.toCharArray()) {
        if(node.map.get(w) == null) {
            TrieNode child = new TrieNode();
            node.map.put(w, child);
        }
        node = node.map.get(w);
        //node reference changed to current node.
    }

    node.isLeaf = true;
}
```

For the word "what" : 'w', 'h', 'a', 't' are inserted character by character. From the childMap of root 'w' is queried. If it's empty, a new TrieNode child is created and inserted into the root map. If the node already exists, the next character continues by assigning nodes with the current character. If there are no more characters left, then the node is marked as a leaf. Same process continues for all the remaining words.

Time complexity : O(m), where m is the word length. In each iteration of the algorithm, we either examine or create a node in the trie till we reach the end of the word.

Space complexity : O(m). In the worst case the newly inserted key doesn't share a prefix with the keys already inserted in the trie. We have to add mm new nodes, which takes us O(m) space.

Search

Search follows similar logic as insert. Each character of the word to be searched is iterated and the node is traversed one by one from the root. If at any instance, there is no node with the character of the search word, it means the word is not present in the word list.

```
/** Returns if the word is in the trie. */
public boolean search(TrieNode root, String word) {
    Trie node = root;
    for(char ch : word.toCharArray()) {
        if(node.map.get(ch) == null) {
            return false;
        }
        node = node.map.get(ch);
    }

    return node.isLeaf;
}

```

AutoSuggestion

Similar approach can be applied to the Auto Suggestion problem. Initially a trie is constructed with all the possible sentences. For the given input prefix, each word is split into separate characters. Similar to trie traversal we saw in search, we can go through each character one by one which means we go level by level for each of the nodes from the root. Once we reach a node which matches our prefix, we look at all the children of the prefix node which is nothing but the branches that we want to do that suggestions. In the tree representation of the sample words, for the input prefix 'wh' we reached the second level node marked 'h'. This node

How to get Suggestions for Top Searched sentences?

We have seen in our Trie that each leaf node represents one full sentence or word. If we have to get the auto suggestions by some *rank* for example, how many times a user has accepted the correct suggestion for the predictions we have shown or how much trending is a specific sentence etc., we can maintain a node level rank at every leaf node.

Considering our previous example, the modified trie for (what, whatsapp, whole, whole foods, demo) can look like below.

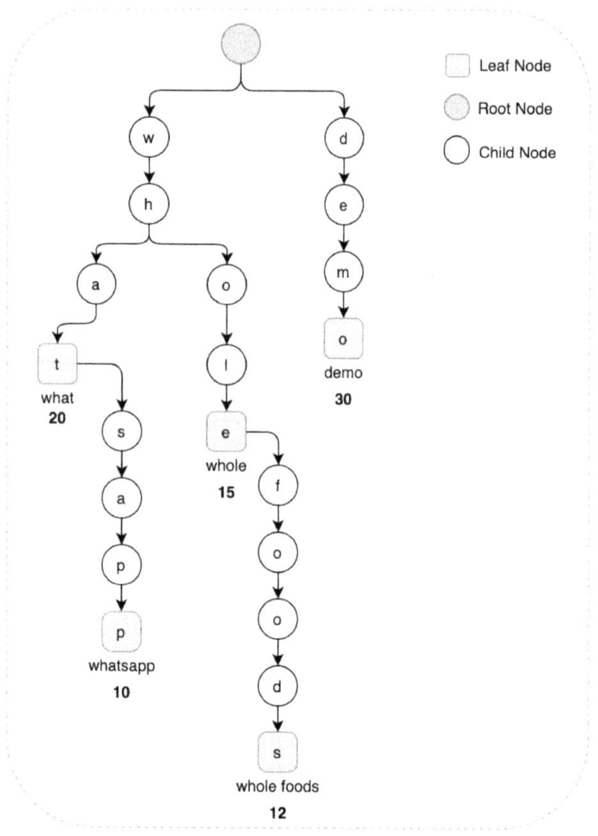

Trie representation with rank for words (what, whatsapp, whole, whole foods, demo)

If you observe the leaf nodes, each of them are tagged with a number eg: what : 20, whatsapp : 10, whole : 15, whole foods : 12 and demo : 30. This number represents the rank of the node. For simplicity let this rank be : how many times a particular sentence is searched. More frequently a sentence is searched, higher the value this rank would be.

Whenever a node is created and updated, this rank value is also updated. When we want to get the list of top N auto suggestions, we will get the list of children sorted by the rank in descending order and provide the first N nodes to the user. For example in the above trie, if a user searches with a prefix "wh" all the children along with their ranks sorted in descending order of"wh" are [what (20), whole (15), whole foods (12), whatsapp (10)]. If we want to show the top 3 auto suggestions, then we can just provide the first three sentences in the above list viz. [what (20), whole (15), whole foods (12)). whatsapp(10) is excluded from the result list.

Can we get the results much faster?

Definitely yes. In the above trie structure we've seen that every time we want to get the top N results, we traverse through the trie, get the leafs and return the result based on the descending order of rank of the leafs. To speed this lookup process, instead of doing the whole computation during the read request, if we can precompute and save the value at each node level, it will drastically improve the performance. Let's look at the modified trie.

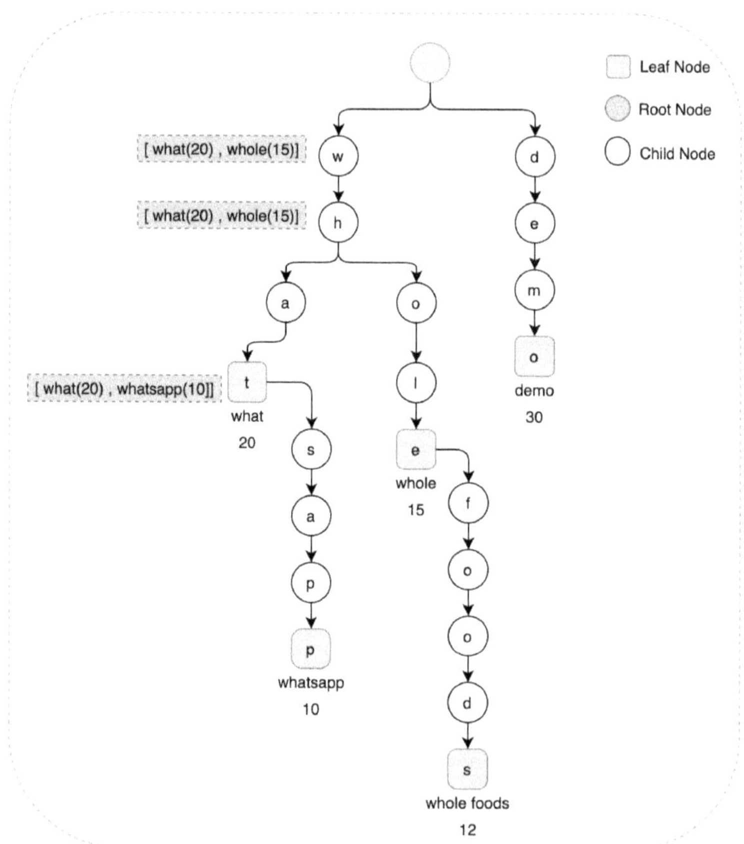

Trie representation with rank + Precomputed frequent words index (what, whatsapp, whole, whole foods, demo)

From the above image, if you look at the sample nodes 'w', 'h', 't' each of these nodes are tagged with precomputed words. Whenever a node is updated we update the rank. At the same time, we need to precompute an array of top N suggestions for a specific node and save it as part of the node payload. So when a new auto suggestion request comes, instead of computing the data at read time, we will just return the values from the precomputed list (computedTopN). The updated Node structure looks like below.

```
class TrieNode {
    Map<Character, TrieNode> childMap;
    boolean amILeaf;
    Long rank;
    List<String> computedTopN;

}
```

For a given node, we can return the top N suggestions from the "**computedTopN**" list.

End to End High Level System Design

With this concept in mind, let's look at the end to end design of our system.

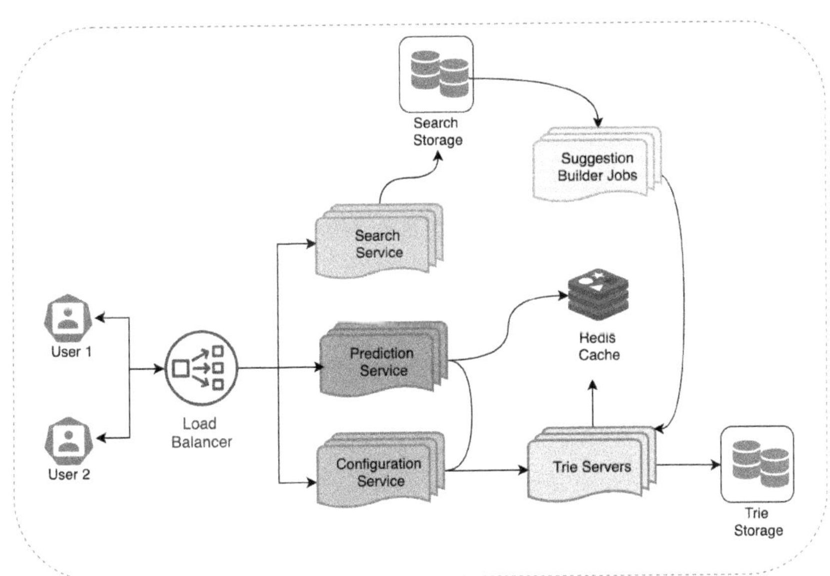

Scalable System design for Search Auto suggestions

If we divide our architecture into a set of microservices with each service having individual responsibilities, the overall services can be as shown in the image.

Read Path

When a user types a prefix we need to give a list of suggestions. This is the typical READ path of our system. Read path involves various services as below.

Prediction Service

When an auto suggestion request comes into the system, it's directed to the prediction service. Prediction service talks to three different components namely Trie Servers, Configuration Service, Cache servers.

1. Trie Servers

Now that we know what a Trie is and how to do auto suggestions, in order to do dynamic auto suggestions we need to maintain the exact tree structure in memory. But storing the whole Trie in a single machine may not be a feasible option because of two reasons

1. Since the number of sentences are very high, the whole trie won't be able to fit in a single machine memory.
2. If a machine goes down, we will lose the entire trie structure.

So we need to maintain the trie itself on multiple servers. To do that we need to partition the tree into smaller chunks. Let's look at various strategies.

Data Partitioning

Partition By Range: We can divide the tree based on each of the substree structures. At level 1 of the tree we get all the subtrees starting with unique characters. So one way to partition our data is to separate the subtree based on the starting letter i.e. All the words that begin with alphabet A goes to server 1, alphabet B goes to server 2 etc. But then english sentences are not distributed equally. In the dictionary itself letter E can have more frequent words than letter Z etc. This brings us to the problem of unequal partitioning i.e. server with letter E tends to have more data than server with letter Z. This doesn't solve our use case fully.

Partition By Server Capacity: In this strategy, we can group all the subtrees under one server as long as the server capacity is not reached. If the memory goes beyond a server capacity we will partition the subtrees after the inserted node. All the subnodes can go to a different server. So if we look at the sentences, the terms such as B to BBC can be in one server. Terms BBD to BBZZ can be on a different server.

This will help us distribute the load equally and is a good fit for our needs. One problem with this approach is that certain sentences are more frequently accessed compared to certain non frequently accessed sentences. Because of this some servers can become hotspots ie. load can be drastically high on certain servers vs some other servers. To avoid this problem, we can distribute the load based on hashing.

Partition By Hash

For every prefix that we receive, we can create a hash to the prefix and store the substree based on the hash function. If we chose the hash function based on Consistent hashing, it's easy for us to redistribute the load. If a hotspot is created for a particular node, we can break down the keys into much smaller servers and recreate the partitions. So essentially we will have a server to range map as below example,

Range A - EBCD : Server 1

Range EBCE - TTAB - Server 2

....

Range ZA - ZZZZ - Server N

So each of the word ranges are assigned to various servers as above.

2. Configuration Service

We now know that each of the trie servers needs to be divided into multiple servers and the respective range configurations has to be stored. Configuration service does the range management for the server cluster. All the requests to the trie servers first goes to the configuration service. If a search term needs to be queried, it first goes to the configuration service and gets the serverId which has the term range. Then it goes to the actual Trie Server and gets the data. Similarly whenever a range needs to be split it is managed by the configuration servers. Zookeeper is a best fit to do dynamic configuration management. Using zookeeper watchers, we can detect if a server is up or down and assign the partition ranges to a new online server.

Trie Storage

So far we have seen that trie structure has to be stored in memory. But what happens to the data if a specific trie server is down? We might end up losing the data if we don't save it anywhere. So we need to have a Trie Storage to permanently persist the trie data for each of the trie servers. Trie storage can be backed by a File system where the exact trie structure can be serialized and stored on a file. Whenever a new server replaces a server, it can read through this file and loads the data into memory. Periodically in memory trie needs to be flushed onto the file for any new updates. Another approach would be to store the structure in a database. We can maintain the node and the node children configuration information in either a SQL database or the modern graph based databases like Neo4j etc to store the trie data. This is a more optimal approach compared to the file approach. This way we are having a fault tolerance into our system.

3. Cache

Server Side Cache

The scale of our system is about ~80K Requests per second. Also the response of autosuggestion requests should come very fast as the user typing speed can be very high. As the user types more letters and more words suggestions should instantly change. To achieve the performance we need it's important to have the data cached as much as possible. For the Trie auto suggestion requests, currently we maintain top N suggestions at each node level. Along with it we need to maintain the data in a distributed caching system like Redis or memcached in order to serve the requests faster. So in our cache we can store the following data.

Prefix	Suggestion List
wh	what, whole
wha	what, whatsapp

Key can be Prefix. Value can be a list of top suggestions for the prefix. We can store the data in the redis key value pairs. So when a user starts searching for a sentence, each time the user enters a letter, the prefix sentence is sent to our Prediction server. Prediction servers check the redis cache if there are any suggestions for a given prefix. If the prefix is found in redis we can retrieve the suggestions values and return to the client. If the data is not found in the redis, we will lookup our Trie Server nodes, fetch the suggestion list and store the list in redis for the prefix and then return the result to the client. This way if someone accesses this prefix in future, it will be served from cache directly.

Client Side Cache

So far we have seen the caching on the server side. If we have to speed up suggestions further we can do the caching at our client side too. Our Mobile app or the website opened on the browser where the user is actually typing for a search query is the client in our case. So whenever a user starts typing for a search query, we can get the results of that query and store it in the client memory i.e. in javascript global cache or browser level local cache or the app storage. If a user types a specific set of searches we can get the results of that search prefix as well as some of the trending search queries similar to the search pattern and store them in the client end. So next time when a user types for some prefix, we can first check if there are any local suggestions and display them. If not found then we can trigger the backend request.

Building Client

Client in our case is either a mobile app or the website opened on a browser.

- Once the user starts typing for the search query, the client will have an "*onKeyUp*" event handler which reads the query each time a keyboard letter press is released.
- Client first checks if this query is in the local client side cache. If it's present, respective suggestions are given. If it's not present then it initiates a Http request to the backend.
- It reads the result from the backend and displays the list to the user as well as store in local cache.
- Clients can wait for the user to enter at least 2 to 3 characters before sending the backend request.
- Clients can pre fetch some of the requests from the server for future requests.

Write Path

So far we have seen the components on the read path i.e. to get a list of suggestions for a prefix. But what about the write path i.e. how to actually build the suggestions for a prefix ? To build the list of suggestions for our service, we will rely on Search service and Suggestion builder jobs.

Search Service

When a user tries to search for some query,

1. First the auto complete suggestions pop up for the given search prefix.
2. Then the user either accepts the auto suggestion or he continues typing and the press enter/search button.

Search service is the core service which serves the actual search results for a given search query. We will not deal with how this service is built at its out of scope of this question. But one important thing to note is that, whenever a user accepts the search auto suggestions, the counter for the prefix vs search suggestion is incremented so that we can recalculate the top N suggestions. Let's say the user continued typing his own sentence without choosing from our suggestion list and then press enter / search button it means the sentence doesn't exist in our Trie. So in this case, since the sentence is not present in the Trie, we will mark the sentence as a new sentence in our Search Storage. Search storage can be one of the sql tables to maintain the list of sentences that are new into the trie.

Suggestion Builder Jobs

So in a day there could be many new search queries that different users can search. Each of these new queries are marked as new queries in the search storage. Periodically once in a few hours or few minutes etc, we can have a set of Scheduled Jobs, let's name them Suggestion Builder jobs whose main goal is to populate the sentences into the trie. Since the sentence is a new sentence, we follow the Trie Insertion algorithm to go from root and then letter by letter in the sentence until we form the child nodes for the search sentence. One interesting point to note is that our trie is distributed into multiple servers. Suggestion Builder jobs should continuously query the configuration management service to the list of servers in which the child nodes are allocated in order to add new indexes into the trie.

5. Final Thoughts and Future Extensibility

Our system is scalable to a large extent with the above approach. If we have to improve it further to accommodate future growth we can have the below modifications.

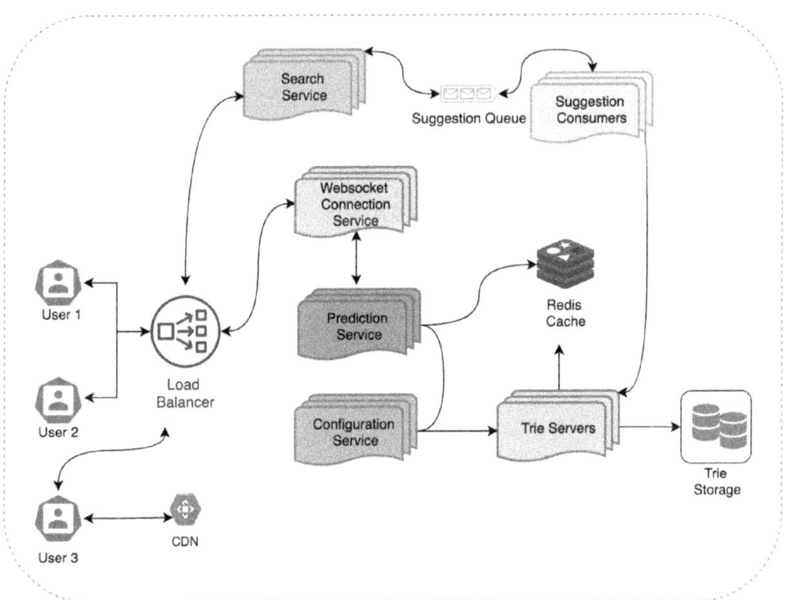

Final Scalable System design for Search Auto suggestions

CDN Cache

As the number of users grow in our system across the globe, we can have a set of CDN servers which will have cached auto suggestion data that are spread across the globe. Whenever a user tries to perform a search query, the request is first sent to the CDN server to see if any relevant sentences exist for the most popular queries. If it's not found then the regular request is placed to the backend server. The main goal is to serve the user requests from the servers that are the closest to the user location so the request travel time can be reduced.

Connection speedup

We have seen that our clients should send a backend HTTP request every time a user releases the key from the keyboard. Sending a HTTP request involves multiple activities like Connection establishment, sending data and receiving the response. Connection establishment is one of the time consuming steps especially when dealing with distributed workload. To avoid this, we can make use of Websockets. Websockets as we discussed in our websockets section, is a bidirectional persistent connection where server and client can be connected to each other for a long time. We can have a separate set of servers as shown in the image above called "Websocket Socket Connection Servers". Our search client can initiate a websocket connection and stay connected for a long time with the server. Every time a user enters a key, we can just send the data to the server via the websocket connection. This process can happen simultaneously as the server processes the initial request. Connection servers manges the whole state of client socket connections. These servers take the request from the client and query the prediction service to get the suggestion list and return the data via the websocket connection. This is one of the fastest ways to avoid HTTP connection roundtrips.

Near Real time search query building

In our service we have seen the "Suggestion Builder Jobs" that run periodically a few times a day to build the trie index. This can cause delay in building the trie. For trending search queries this may not be an optimal approach. Instead we can have distributed queues called "Suggestion Queues". Whenever a search server detects a new query, it can push the query into a Suggestion Queues. There can be a set of dedicated processes called "Suggestion Consumer" which will continuously listen to the suggestion queues and populate the trie as well the respective indexes. This makes sure the Trie index is almost real time.

Analytics

We can have a set of analytics that we can run in the backend to detect some of the trending search queries and user query patterns. These analytics can be used to build the rank of each of the search queries and the suggestion lists can be updated based on the analytics results.

As always system design is a very vast topic and each of the systems can be designed in multiple ways. This is one way to solve the Auto suggestions problem. There could be other better approaches that may be used in the real world, but the underlying concepts will be almost the same as we just discussed. Try your own design and share it with the world.

Final Thoughts

As you traverse the challenging landscape of system design interviews, success depends not only on technical prowess but also on a strategic mindset and continual improvement. Let these guiding principles illuminate your path forward.

Mindset is the Key to Success

Your mindset shapes your approach to challenges and ultimately determines your success. Approach system design interviews with a growth mindset, embracing challenges as opportunities for learning and growth. Cultivate resilience, adaptability, and a positive attitude to overcome obstacles and achieve your goals.

Focus on Weak Areas and Improve Iteratively

Identify your weak areas and commit to improving them iteratively.

Remember failures are not opposite to success. Instead they are together with success.

Continuously seek feedback, iterate on your solutions, and refine your problem-solving skills to become a more effective system designer.

Learn Through Observation in Real-World Systems

Take every opportunity to observe and learn from real-world systems. Analyze existing systems, study their architectures, and identify design patterns and best practices. Draw insights from real-world examples to inform your approach to system design interviews and deepen your understanding of complex concepts.

Join Our System Design Preparation Group

In order to have a helping hand as you prepare for system design interviews, we have started a support group to collaborate with like-minded individuals, share insights and experiences, and support each other on your path to success. Together, we can elevate our skills, overcome challenges, and achieve our goals in system design interviews.

To join you can visit https://pramod.me/

Cheat Sheet for Rough Capacity Estimations

(Latest cheatsheet with regular updates can be found at https://pramod.me/)

Calculations for convenience:

To save time during system design, try to approximate as much as possible to nearly rounded numbers.

~ symbol represents 'Approximate' data.

1 day = 24 * 60 * 60 = 86,400 sec = ~90,000 sec

1Million/day = ~11.5/sec = ~10/sec

10 Million/day = ~115/sec = ~100/sec

1Billion/day = ~11574/sec = ~11K/sec = ~10K/sec

1 Million = 1,000,000 = 10 ^ 6

1 Billion = 1,000,000,000 = 10 ^ 9 = 1000 Million

Data type sizes: (Based on java)

Char = 1 byte

Short = 2 bytes

Int = 4 bytes

Long = 8 bytes

Boolean = 1 bit

DateTime/Timestamp = 10 bytes

1TB = 1000GB

1GB = 1000MB = 10 ^9

1MB = 1000KB = 10 ^ 6

1KB = 1000B = 10 ^ 3

1B = 8 bits

About the Author

Gopala Krishna Murty Nanduri brings a fresh perspective on system design interviews, shaped by his transition from a distinguished government career to the field of software engineering. His unique approach simplifies

complex system design concepts into clear, easy-to-understand solutions.

No matter if you're a student, early-career professional, or mid-career switcher, his explanation and insights make mastering system design concepts straightforward, proving that with the right guidance, anyone can succeed in even the most challenging technical interviews.

To help you being successful in System design interviews or general interview preparation, join our online group at https://pramod.me/system-design